BREAKING
controlling powers

Victory over Spiritual Attacks

A Collection of Three Best-Selling Books

BREAKING
controlling powers

Victory over Spiritual Attacks

A Collection of Three Best-Selling Books

ROBERTS
Liardon

WHITAKER
HOUSE

BREAKING CONTROLLING POWERS:
A COLLECTION OF THREE BEST-SELLING BOOKS
Includes *Breaking Controlling Powers, Learning to Say No without Feeling Guilty,* and *How to Survive an Attack*

Roberts Liardon Ministries
P.O. Box 30710
Laguna Hills, CA 92654

ISBN-13: 978-0-88368-554-9
ISBN-10: 0-88368-554-X
Printed in the United States of America
© 2000 by Roberts Liardon Ministries

1030 Hunt Valley Circle
New Kensington, PA 15068
www.whitakerhouse.com

Library of Congress Cataloging-in-Publication Data
Liardon, Roberts.
Breaking controlling powers : a collection of three best-selling books / Roberts Liardon.
p.   cm.
Summary: "Compilation of three of Liardon's works (How to Survive an Attack, Breaking Controlling Powers, and How to Say No without Feeling Guilty) that deal with taking charge of your life"—Provided by publisher.
ISBN-13: 978-0-88368-554-9 (pbk. : alk. paper)
ISBN-10: 0-88368-554-X (pbk. : alk. paper)
1. Spiritual warfare. I. Liardon, Roberts. How to survive an attack. II. Liardon, Roberts. Learning how to say no without feeling guilty. III. Title: How to survive an attack. IV. Title: Learning how to say no without feeling guilty. V. Title.
BV4509.5.L52 2005
248.4—dc22   2005014416

1 2 3 4 5 6 7 8 9 10 11 ᴜᴌ 11 10 09 08 07 06 05

BOOK ONE

BREAKING CONTROLLING POWERS

7

BOOK TWO

LEARNING TO SAY NO WITHOUT FEELING GUILTY

101

BOOK THREE

HOW TO SURVIVE AN ATTACK

157

ABOUT THE AUTHOR

265

BREAKING CONTROLLING POWERS

CONTENTS

BREAKING CONTROLLING POWERS

1. What Is Control? 11
2. Abusive Control 14
3. Emotional Manipulation 18
4. Spiritual Manipulation 26
5. Abusive Control in the Bible 39
6. Positive, Justifiable Control 51
7. Positive, Biblical Control 60
8. Are You a Controller? 66
9. Control by Parents 76
10. Control by Spouses 81
11. Control by Money 87
12. How to Be Free from Control 94

CHAPTER

ONE

WHAT IS CONTROL?

Control seems to be a problem in every time of transition from an old wave of God's glory to a new wave—such as we are experiencing today. The power of control affects every circle of Christianity. The abuse of control holds people in unnecessary bondage and hinders them from fulfilling the purpose of God in their lives.

Some people exert a natural control over others. Individuals can exercise self-control from within. But a demonic control can also be exercised by one person over another.

While this book will deal with the abuse of control, we will also examine the positive side of control, which is called commitment. This God-given authority is placed on an individual who is committed to fulfill the plan of God in the earth and who looks to the Lord, not to people, personal security, or promotion.

Each of us needs to exercise self-control in order to keep ourselves free from sin. We exercise this control by applying the Word of God to our lives. The Word is the balance, and we must all use discipline in our daily experiences. But people who exercise abusive control seek to become the deciding factors in the lives of others. Such individuals replace the Word of God as the balance in the lives of those whom they dominate, and they react negatively if they are not the controlling factor in all decisions made.

We must realize that what happens in the spiritual realm is reflected in the natural realm. A great struggle goes on in the world today for control of people's minds. This struggle is between the forces of light (Christianity) and the forces of the darkness (satanic powers).

Although Communism has deteriorated, the people of the world suffered enormously as a result of the ungodly natural control exercised by Communist control. Such totalitarian governments dominate people through fear, ignorance, and poverty, restricting their knowledge of the outside world and limiting their freedom of expression and religion.

A great struggle goes on in the world today for control of people's minds.

At the time of this writing, I have traveled to some forty nations of the world, including some that have been under, and some that are still influenced by, Communist rule. So I am writing from firsthand knowledge of the conditions that exist, not only in the church world, but also in society in general. In Communist states, I have lain in the back of a truck while live bullets rushed over my head. In these nations some people were killed because of their desire for political, economic, and religious freedom. I have seen the bread lines, and I have heard Christians in the underground churches voice the anguish of their lives.

However, people living in free societies are not immune to abusive control. This control may come from well-meaning parents, spouses, friends, creditors, spiritual leaders, even children. The purpose of this book is to help Christians recognize the core of the problem of abusive control and to understand its negative actions and reactions so they can be set free themselves and effectively minister to those who are still in bondage.

It is also important to recognize and understand the positive side of control. When we do, we can accurately discern the difference between abusive and positive control, submit to proper authority, and grow into full maturity in the body of Christ.

CHAPTER

TWO

ABUSIVE CONTROL

Sometimes it is necessary to isolate, reveal, and understand the negative side of an issue in order to properly discern its positive side. In learning to operate in the realm of the spirit, we usually learn the correct methods of operation by trial and error. When we make a mistake, we correct it, make the proper adjustment, and go on. Defining the problem is important because it helps to determine the solution. This is true in the area of abusive control.

Control does not originate in strangers. The devil does not use a passerby on the street to control the life of an individual Christian or the church of Jesus Christ. Please understand that principle. If a stranger walked into your home or down the aisle of your church, announcing that he had come on the premises to take over, you would throw him out. But if someone you know and trust were to come on the scene for the same purpose, because of your personal respect for him, you would not be so quick to eject him.

At some point in the future, some of the people you respect right now may decide not to go on following the Lord. If you are not secure in the Lord yourself, this situation could cause a great problem in your life, your destiny, and your church. You must find your source of being in God and be able to discern accurately in the Spirit.

DEFINITION OF ABUSIVE CONTROL

Let's begin our study by answering this question: What is abusive control?

Abusive control can be defined as "an attempt to dominate another person in order to fulfill one's own desires and to enhance personal security." The individual who exercises abusive control has no personal regard or consideration for the one being controlled and dominated. The *abusive controller* may be a child, an adult, a spouse, a brother or sister, a parent or grandparent, an employee, a student, a church member, a leader, or a best friend. The controller's goal is survival, at any cost.

CHARACTERISTICS OF THE ABUSIVE CONTROLLER

An abusive controller is insecure. Although such a person may appear to handle everything with ease and confidence, deep inside this person is scared, intimidated, and unfulfilled.

Fear of rejection is the motivating force behind the actions of an abusive controller. Although a controller may seem to be a person we can depend upon, in truth that person is the dependent one. Manipulation of others is important for this person to feel needed, and it provides him with a feeling of security.

Whenever we place our security in something or someone other than God, and God alone, we open ourselves to deception, defeat, and despair. It is true that we need others to help encourage and sharpen us, but our dependency should be upon God, not people. We should never base our lives on the opinions of others around us. We should compare *people's words* with *God's words* and follow the leading and direction of the Lord.

Abusive controllers are obsessed with supervising the behavior of others. Their entire focus is on someone or something other than themselves. They cannot define the direction or describe the plan for their own lives because they are so wrapped up in the person they are controlling. Whenever our security lies in something or someone other than God, it will fail.

Our dependency should be on God, not people.

Abusive controllers stifle the creative move of the Spirit through the persons under their power. Because they are bound by fear, they hinder the ability of others to be themselves. Many abusive controllers have a genuine desire to see the move of God operate accurately and successfully. But in attempting to promote that move, they can become religious and smother the true call and gifts of those around and under them. They usually avoid open expressions of feelings and direct, honest communication.

Because of fear of rejection, abusive controllers have selfish personalities. Controllers make demands easily and, many times, express these demands ruthlessly. Abusive controllers have a low sense of self-worth. These people have abandoned the problems within and have turned their entire focus on the problems of others. Fed by a sense of personal rejection, controllers base their lives and the results on what they can accomplish through their own works. They look at those around them as their own accomplishments. If the people they control fail, they feel that they are failures.

Please understand that rejection has nothing to do with self-worth. Rejection is a strong, demonic spirit in the world. Whether we are accepted or rejected by others has nothing to do with our value or worth as children of God.

NATURE OF ABUSIVE CONTROL

Abusive control is a sense of power used by the devil to deceive the one who wields it. God Himself gave humankind a free will, and He will not violate our gift of choice and decision. God is the God of reality.

Abusive control is undermining and, many times, secretive. It is accompanied by unnatural attachment, and every relationship it touches crumbles in destruction. Finally, manipulation characterizes abusive control; it is the main tool of the abusive controller, who uses it to keep others in bondage to him. In the following two chapters we will discuss the primary areas of abusive control: emotional and spiritual manipulation.

CHAPTER
3
THREE

EMOTIONAL MANIPULATION

However we may evaluate abusive control, it still finds its source in a reactionary process. An abusive controller will either overreact or underreact—whichever it takes to keep his victim suspended. This happens because an abusive controller finds fulfillment in the soulish realm.

The soulish realm produces a false sense of security, giving ground to the work of demonic spirits. Instead of finding and fulfilling his rightful place of commitment and security in Christ Jesus, an abusive controller attempts to pamper himself and others through the use of personal power and unnatural respect.

TYPES OF EMOTIONAL MANIPULATION

The principal method used by an abusive controller is emotional manipulation. Tears, claims of helplessness, anger, threats, and silence are all primary instruments of emotional manipulation. Silence, which is a form of rejection, is an especially powerful emotional tool.

Many people become controlled by their own emotions because they make their decisions primarily based on feelings. This is precisely why they make so many wrong decisions. In fact, many Christians make the mistake of deciding by feelings rather than by the leadership of the Holy Spirit. Finding security in Jesus is the deciding factor between feelings and accurate direction by the Holy Spirit.

> **By basing decisions on feelings, people are controlled by emotions.**

Feeling-based decisions are the primary reason behind young people choosing the wrong marriage partner, leading to unhappiness and, often, divorce. They are why some career people end up making wrong business decisions, losing everything they own. They are why many a servant of God is filling the wrong pulpit. (Just because a congregation is nice to a minister does not mean that he is called to become their pastor!)

TEARS AND HELPLESSNESS

A classic example of emotional manipulation starts when both sets of parents want a recently married couple to spend the Christmas holidays with them. It begins innocently enough when the bride mentions to her mother, "I think we are going to John's parents' for Christmas."

The mother starts crying and complaining, "You don't love us anymore or you would come to our house for the holidays!" This negative reaction throws the daughter into an emotional state. She wavers and finally agrees to change their plans.

But when the husband calls his mother with the news, she is equally upset and adamant. "But we have everything all planned!" she wails. "We can't possibly change things now!"

Many people are controlled through such displays of emotion. It happens not only to newlyweds but to people in every stage of life. Often, when someone doesn't agree with the controlling person, the controller will start whining, "You don't love me," or, "You don't want me around anymore."

Not all abusive controllers rule with an iron hand. Some come clothed in sweetness and gentleness. These particular controllers are lethal. If they can't manifest a tear, they will sometimes revert to helplessness. Their intention is to make their victim feel an overwhelming sense of responsibility to them and to their lives. Such controllers know how to play on the strings of guilt and pity. They control through their supposed sickness, weakness, and victimization. Although their ailments or infirmities are sometimes legitimate, more often they are fabricated or at least exaggerated. These people make their victims feel that if they do not pamper and pet them, their whole world will crumble.

> **Be gentle but firm. Do not allow yourself to be emotionally manipulated.**

Do you know what you should do if you find yourself being exploited by this type of abusive controller? Be gentle but firm. Let that person know that you will not allow yourself to be emotionally manipulated.

If someone tries to make you feel obligated to change your long-established plans just to suit his or her selfish desires, say to that person, "My feelings for you have nothing to do with the circumstances. I am sorry that you are upset, but this is just the way things are." If a sympathy-seeking exploiter misuses and abuses you, just tell him or her, "I don't like it when you act this way. You are not respecting me." Sometimes you may have to be blunt and say, "I don't have to agree with you in this area and be manipulated by your attitude."

Don't fall into the trap of emotional manipulation by thinking that something is wrong with you. Judge yourself by the Word of God. If you have peace within, then know that the emotional outburst of the other person is an indication of his or her problem or present circumstance and not a reflection of you.

ANGER

If a display of tears and helplessness won't work, often a controlling person will retreat into anger—and most people do not know how to handle an individual who is angry.

Do you know what to do with an angry person? Just stay calm. Do not react with anger. If you react by losing your temper, it fuels the other person's anger. If you feed the flame, an entire chain of negative events could be set off. Don't do anything that might provoke or justify improper behavior. Look at the angry person, state the truth calmly and quietly, and refuse to react negatively. By refusing to react in anger, you remove yourself from the power of this type of abusive control.

Learn to stop reacting in ways that are not necessary and do not work. Sometimes it is good to leave an angry person alone with his rage. An angry individual may not know what to do in that situation. He may hit the wall and beat on a chair. If he does, leave the room until he has calmed down. When you come back into the room, simply say to him, "Why did you punch a hole in my wall? Can we discuss the problem like adults?"

Understand that when you disarm an abusive controller, extreme emotions will surface. Anger will monopolize the atmosphere, as well as your thoughts, if you are not careful. Angry words will hit your mind like machine gun bullets, preventing you from defending yourself properly.

Keep your perspective clear and precise. When you make a choice to live responsibly, others must live that way also.

THREATS

Words of failure, defeat, unnatural obligation, guilt, criticism, and intimidation often follow. These threats are all used in an attempt to control a person's life. They are designed to paralyze a person with fear.

The Bible has much to say about the power of words:

Death and life are in the power of the tongue: and they that love it shall eat the fruit thereof. (Proverbs 18:21)

Scripture refers to words as "swords" (Psalm 59:7; Hebrews 4:12; Revelation 1:16, 19:15, for example), and those words spoken negatively in our lives will have an adverse effect if we receive them and live according to them. The *Amplified Bible* version of Psalm 55:21 says,

The words of his mouth were smoother than cream or butter, but war was in his heart; his words were softer than oil, yet they were drawn swords.

Again, the *Amplified Bible* has this interpretation of Psalm 59:7:

Behold, they belch out [insults] with their mouths; swords [of sarcasm, ridicule, slander, and lies] are in their lips, for who, they think, hears us?

Just as a sword or an arrow pierces the heart on a battlefield, so negative words are designed to pierce the heart of the hearer. If words are spoken negatively and abusively, they will wound. They will hurt deeply if they are not removed. No one can carry negative words in his heart and still fulfill the plan and purpose of God for his life, just as he cannot walk around with a sword or an arrow thrust in his chest and live long!

Here is an example of threatening words. Suppose you announce in full assurance that God has called you to leave your home and loved ones behind and to go serve Him in a far-off place. An abusive controller will reply by saying, "You'll never make it there," or, "You'll probably die there." Sometimes he or she will threaten your relationship by responding, "If you go, don't ever contact me again," or, "If you go, you will not be welcome in this house anymore." Financial threats might even be used:

How do you remove abusive words from your heart? With the Word of God.

"If you go, I will not send you any more money," or, "If you go, you will go broke and starve." Such words are an attack against you! Words of failure and defeat dominate the lives of many people without their even being aware of it.

How do you "pull" these negative, abusive words out of your heart? By counterattacking them with the Word of God. The first half of Hebrews 4:12 AMP tells us,

> For the Word that God speaks is alive and full of power [making it active, operative, energizing, and effective]; it is sharper than any two-edged sword.

Speak the Word of God over yourself. Scripture says that the Word of God is *"sharper than any two-edged sword."* The accurate Word will calm and heal the wounds of abusive words. Negative words can affect your life only if you allow them to do so.

SILENCE

If tears, anger, and threats will not work, then the controlling person will attempt to use silence as a weapon. He will shut out his victim by ignoring him and keeping him dangling, wondering what the controller is thinking and how he is feeling. Those who are weak in spirit cannot handle such treatment. That is why weak people are so easily controlled.

If someone is trying to control you by using silence, what should you do? Nothing! Let that individual be silent! Go on with your business and your life. Don't let silence control your activities and make you nervous. Don't get into turmoil because of what someone else is doing or not doing. Make a choice to live in joy and contentment.

> **Don't get into turmoil because of what someone else is doing or not doing.**

Sometimes in a church, an elder or a deacon will resort to this kind of manipulation against the pastor. If this happens, the pastor should confront the issue. If the controlling person will not respond, repent, and change, the pastor should remove him from the board until he shows evidence of spiritual growth and maturity.

AVOID DEPENDENCE ON ANOTHER

Do not be overly dependent on other people. Do not expect others to pray on your behalf and get answers from heaven for you. It doesn't matter how spiritual you think they are or how accurate they have been in the past. Godly counsel is good, but if you direct your life and future according to the word of another, you are setting yourself up for control and misery.

You must hear from God for yourself, then season the godly counsel of others who have proven themselves with God's Word. God has a plan for your life. He may mature that plan through others, but He will not lead you through another. Fear will cause you to depend upon another person. The Bible says that the Holy Spirit is our Guide. He will lead from within.

If you are a dependent person, you cannot enjoy normal fellowship with others because your joy, happiness, and thoughts will come from them—not from how God sees the real you.

CHAPTER
4
FOUR

SPIRITUAL MANIPULATION

In discussing abusive control, please note that the area of spiritual manipulation is by far the most dangerous. It is dangerous for both the controller and the one being controlled because it treads on the spiritual principles of heaven. Like emotional manipulation, spiritual manipulation is based on the soulish realm. It has nothing to do with the true spiritual realm. It is still soulish maneuvering, but it uses a spiritual principle as its primary tool.

By recalling the attributes of an abusive controller, we can see many reasons why such a person would revert to spiritual manipulation. If an individual cannot control another person through emotions, he will refer to a "higher power"—a form of spiritual manipulation—to keep his victim subservient to him. Spiritual manipulators have not developed godly character in a particular area. Their lust or desire for control leads them rather than the Spirit of God.

In 1 Timothy 3:2, 6, we read these words: *"A bishop then must be blameless,....not a novice, **lest being lifted up with pride** he fall into the condemnation of the devil"* (emphasis added).

The apostle Paul wrote this passage to warn Timothy against allowing a young, inexperienced convert to assume the responsibilities of spiritual leadership. Paul knew the danger of promoting too quickly those who had not yet spiritually matured. Such people often fall prey to the temptation of pride. They tend to get "puffed up" if the church gives them a high position. Instead of humbly serving the body of Christ, they become pious and manipulative.

On some, God has truly bestowed a special anointing or gift. Again, if they have not fully matured, often such people will feel that they are among the elite and will carry an air of superiority about them. They will look down on others whom they consider to be less spiritual than they are and will often use or abuse those under their authority rather than loving and caring for them. Such people fail to recognize that a strong, godly character helps

God has no superstars; He only has servants.

their gift or anointing to operate at its full potential and to last a lifetime. Those who don't concentrate on building a strong character may lose what gift and anointing they have been given.

God has no superstars; He only has servants. If a servant does his job, God will promote him. But no matter how great his name may become, a true servant will still have a desire to meet the needs of the people in his charge and to help them when they are in trouble. That is what a ministry gift is for. The true servant must be careful not to use his God-given authority to lord it over others.

God is a personal God who speaks to the hearts of men and women individually. Believers who are in leadership roles must be particularly careful to say exactly what the Lord tells them to say—nothing more and nothing less! Leaders have a responsibility to make certain that when they say that something is of God, it really is. They do this by spending time in prayer, by searching the Scriptures, and by seeking seasoned, godly counsel.

CONTROL BY THE SUPER-SPIRITUAL

It never fails: In every church there are members who think everyone should obey them because they have been there the longest or because they are the most spiritual. Either such people will seek to dominate the leadership in every decision made or they will give their advice on everyone's personal life.

Do not base your life on the opinions of another person, especially if that individual has not been ordained by God for leadership. Line up every statement you hear against the Word of God. According to Romans 8:16, we will know the voice of the Lord by our inner witness, not by the soulish feelings or opinions of others.

These super-spiritual people watch for those over whom they can exercise spiritual manipulation. If you have a spiritual call upon your life, they will recognize it and will single you out for their special ministry. Many times such super-spiritual people are unseasoned themselves, so they will give you words from the Lord that will push you out ahead of God's perfect timing. If you are led more strongly by ambition than by the Spirit of God, you will fall for such illusions. Many genuine calls upon people's lives have been aborted because of super-spiritual, abusive controllers.

How do these people abort calls? There are several ways.

One way abusive controllers try to abort divine calls is by acting very spiritual. They act as though they are spiritual people, but in reality their control is of the devil.

Another way is by organizing a Bible study with someone other than the pastor as leader because "the pastor does not teach the *deep* things of the Spirit." Not only does this spell trouble (especially if you are the one chosen to lead this special Bible study), but this kind of behavior is also the core for a church split.

Don't fall prey to this type of spiritual delusion. If it is time for you to be in a position of leadership, God will put you on the field or He will motivate the pastor to invite you to lead a segment of the body—under his supervision. Take your training very seriously, and do not allow yourself to be pushed out ahead of God's timetable by an ambitious controller who wants to take the credit for your success.

> **Do not allow yourself to be pushed out ahead of God's timetable.**

Another way abusive controllers abort calls is by giving out false words from the Lord or false visions. Usually such words or visions are either extremely morbid or extremely favorable. They are designed for the same purpose: to push the hearer out ahead of God's timing and ultimately to abort the call of God upon his life.

The truth is, people who give out such words and visions have not had a visitation from God. Beware of giving heed to such self-styled prophets. When it comes to your personal call, why would God speak something to someone else that He has not already shared with you? Personal prophecies and visions concerning another person are to be a *confirmation* of what the individual already knows in his heart. If another person can entirely lead your life through prophecies and visions, you will never be a leader for God.

The Word of God is very strong against false prophecies and visions. The prophet Jeremiah faced this same kind of situation in his day and cut through the deceit of the religious controllers. (See Jeremiah 23.) In essence he said to them, "You people prophesy out of *your own hearts*. You say that you have received a vision from the Lord when in reality it was just in *your own heads*. You are telling people that there is going to be peace when there is really going to be war. And you are assuring them that they are fine when they are actually guilty of worshipping themselves. You are prophesying falsely. You are speaking out of your own hearts rather than out of the heart of heaven. To you the Lord says, 'I am against you, and you shall be judged.'"

Do not fall into the trap of receiving false words or visions. To be a leader who follows God, you must know the Lord for yourself. You must exercise His character in order to hear His plan for your life and follow His perfect timing.

The devil wants to destroy your calling and thwart your purpose in the earth. His plan of attack will be based on your weaknesses. He will attempt to execute that plan in the way that you least expect, and he will succeed unless you are sensitive to the Spirit of God.

CONTROLLING PRAYERS

Another variation of spiritual manipulation is *controlling prayers*. Can Christians pray controlling prayers? Certainly they can! But if misused, these prayers are a form of witchcraft! As we studied in Chapter 2, the Bible says that our words are like swords and that they contain power. Remember: *Words are spiritual weapons.*

A controlling prayer is composed of words with a spiritual force behind them, spoken to influence the course of another's life. The only time a controlling prayer should be used by a Christian is when the Word and the Spirit of God are used to come against the enemy. Jesus explained this method of prayer in binding and loosing the plan of God against the devil's will. (See Matthew 16:19.)

> **The Bible says our words are like swords. They contain power.**

An abusive controller prays his own human desires or will for someone else out of his own human heart. He is trying to make the other individual obey his selfish desires rather than the Lord's will for that person's life. The person praying may or may not understand that he is loosing evil influences in the spirit realm. A controlling prayer is harmful and misused when it violates or dominates another person's will. Then it becomes a form of witchcraft. In other words, through prayer in the spirit realm, an abusive controller looses demonic influence to control the natural life of another person for the controller's own benefit.

For example, Jesus had just healed a man possessed with a blind and mute evil spirit. The people started to murmur among themselves, for they could not believe the miracle they had just witnessed. In response, Jesus began to teach them about the power of words. He said to them, *"For by your words you will be justified and acquitted, and by your words you will be condemned and sentenced"* (Matthew 12:37 AMP).

With our words we can bless or curse. Controlling prayers fall under the category of "curse," because they are words spoken against other people in an attempt to satisfy selfish human desires.

An example of a controlling prayer is the one prayed by a mother who does not approve of the girl some young man is dating. She wants him to marry her daughter instead, so she prays that the romance will fail and that he will choose her daughter as his bride. I know of a particular case very much like this. A mother prayed and prayed that a young married couple would get a divorce so the husband would "see the light" and marry her daughter. This mother's unceasing, soulish prayers sent trouble into this marriage by her words. Finally the couple became aware of the situation. They rose up and broke the power of the words spoken against them in the spirit realm, and their marriage continued to prosper.

Soulish prayers can occur in any area of life where human desire is placed over the will of God. One of the most commonly misquoted Scriptures in the Bible, often used with soulish prayers, is Psalm 37:4, which reads, *"Delight thyself also in the LORD; and he shall give thee the desires of thine heart."*

I cannot count how many times I have heard this verse quoted by Christians who have placed their own desires over the will of God for their lives—and expected to have those selfish desires fulfilled.

In examining this verse in its true context, we will see an interesting aspect of it that is totally different from the way it is usually interpreted by most believers. In Strong's concordance, we see that the meaning of the Hebrew word translated *"delight"* in this passage is "to be soft or pliable."[1]

---

[1] James Strong, *The Exhaustive Concordance of the Bible* (Nashville: Abingdon, 1890) "Hebrew and Chaldee Dictionary," p. 89, H#6026.

The point the psalmist made in this passage is that when a person "delights" himself in the Lord, he allows God to reform his heart, making it soft and pliable to His will and His purpose. If we truly delight ourselves in the Lord, then our wills are transformed so that it is His desire we seek and not our own. When we fully and completely delight ourselves in God, our soulish desires must change and our hearts become united with His heart. Once we are in that place of softness and submission, we learn to trust Him totally in every area of our lives.

> **When a person delights himself in the Lord, God reforms his heart.**

In Psalm 37:4 the psalmist spoke of a complete "heart transplant," in which we turn our wills over to the Lord, seeking His will and trusting Him to lead us in the way that He wants us to go. Our desires conform to His desire—then we are promised that we shall have the (godly) desires of our hearts.

Spiritual manipulators twist Scriptures to give substance to their controlling prayers. They do not have the heart of God in any situation. *They* want to be God and to make *their* plans work. Spiritual controllers think they know what is best for everyone involved. Since they do not have the heart of God, they cannot know the will of God.

DON'T FEAR THEM

Although soulish, controlling prayers can trouble our lives, we do not need to fear them or become paranoid about them. We only need to be aware of them. They cannot succeed in lives that are *totally* committed to God.

The prayers that are most effective are *fervent prayers.* It is impossible for a controlling prayer to be truly fervent.

The word *fervent* does not mean "desperate," nor does it mean "intense" or "unceasing." In James 5:16 we read these words: *"The effectual fervent prayer of a righteous man availeth much."*

Years ago, the Lord took me to this verse and caused the word *fervent* to stand out to me. I asked myself what it meant to be fervent. As I began to study this verse, I came to Matthew 12:25 which helped me understand why a fervent prayer prevails with God:

And Jesus knew their thoughts, and said unto them, Every kingdom divided against itself is brought to desolation; and every city or house divided against itself shall not stand.

You, as an individual, are a "kingdom" made up of three parts: a spirit, a soul, and a body. Therefore, you are not just a mind or a desire; you are a *spirit* that owns a *mind* and lives in a *body.* Your mind and your body are pieces of equipment that are needed in order for your spirit to carry out the purpose of God in the earth. If you do not properly understand the equipment you have been given, you cannot pray effectively.

The plans of heaven come to you through your spirit.

In prayer, God does not talk to a piece of your equipment—the mind! The Lord speaks to your heart—your spirit man—the *real* you. The plans of heaven come to you through your spirit. That is how God will communicate with you. Your mind may find out a few seconds later and be able to interpret what your spirit has received. That is why your spirit sometimes knows something, but you are not able to put it into words because your mind has not yet comprehended it.

If the three parts of your kingdom are divided, you will not be able to pray effectively, and you will fail. If your spirit is not leading, you are divided.

In fervent prayer your spirit, soul, and body go together into the arena of prayer and worship. Your spirit, soul, and body are as one, united in the purpose of God to see His plan fulfilled, His will done. Your spirit is your source of prayer, and your soul (desires, emotions, imaginations, memories) and body (actions) work together and submit to it.

A person who prays controlling prayers is not "together" no matter how spiritual he may act. He prays from his desire rather than from his spirit. Spiritual manipulators move strongly in the soulish realm, and they will reap a soulish result. A spiritual controller faces three different directions. He can go by the body way or the head way, but he usually avoids the spirit way because it involves a cost—total subjection of personal will to the will of God. Controlling prayers are born from worry, frustration, and flesh. The Bible indicates that because desire, and not the spirit, is the core of their thrust, such prayers represent a house divided and will fail.

In Proverbs 26:2 we are told, *"As the bird by wandering, as the swallow by flying, so the curse causeless shall not come."*

Again, in *Strong's Exhaustive Concordance of the Bible* we see that the Hebrew word translated *"causeless"* means "devoid of cost."[2] The consequence of spiritual carelessness is a door open to the enemy who can use others to harm us through our bodies, our souls, or our spirits.

---

[2] James Strong, *Strong's Exhaustive Concordance of the Bible* (Nashville: Abingdon, 1890) "Hebrew and Chaldee Dictionary," p. 41, H#2600.

The reverse is also true for a strong believer. You need not be concerned about controlling prayers if you are following the will of God and fulfilling His purpose, seasoning yourself in the Word and developing in godly character. The Bible indicates that if your heart has taken on the will of God for your life, you are "paying the price." Proverbs 26:2 says that any words spoken against you will not destroy you if they are spoken by someone who has not "paid the price" (borne the cost) to know God and His ways and character, like you have. (See Psalm 91:3, 5.)

As a believer, you can prevail against any soulish prayers that hinder you. Put the Word of God into practice in your life. Develop a strong sensitivity to the Holy Spirit and His timing in every area. Be committed to godly character and bold integrity. These principles produce security in Him and enable you to follow as He leads you.

> **As a believer, you can prevail against any soulish prayers that hinder you.**

CONTROL BY SPIRITUAL GIFTS

Unfortunately, some can even misuse their gifts in a public setting to control others. Suppose you are in a lively gospel meeting. Everyone is rejoicing and shouting and praising God. All of a sudden someone raises his hands and yells, "Thus saith the Lord." He then delivers a supposed prophecy. (Read 1 Corinthians 14 for a detailed study of the proper functioning of the gifts of the Spirit in public gatherings.)

In every gospel meeting there are all sorts of people present, and each one operates from a different level of spiritual maturity. We must learn to mature ourselves in the Spirit and hear the voice of the Lord accurately. We must not accept an operation of the Spirit just because the majority of the people seem to be ecstatic about it. Do not follow the *mood* of the people; follow the *move* of the Holy Spirit.

After the person has given the prophecy, everyone in the meeting screams, "Yes!" But your spirit says, "No!" If you are not strong in the spirit, you may be swayed by such hyper-flesh moves and prophecies.

Why would the majority accept such a prophecy as from the Lord? One of the reasons is that some have been mesmerized by spiritual gifts instead of being influenced by godly character. Some people become so awed by an exciting display that they do not stop to discern what is true and what is false. They do not realize that Jesus taught that we will know the servants of God by their fruits, not by their gifts. (See Matthew 7:20.)

> **Do not follow the mood of people; follow the move of the Holy Spirit.**

I am not discounting the gifts of God in any way, for they are priceless to the body of Christ. However, we must mature in the realm of the Spirit. We must understand the character of God so we can know when the gifts are in true operation.

One of the attributes of the Holy Spirit is that He will always exalt Jesus—not another human being. I have been in meetings in which the eyes of the people were called continually to focus on the man of God and how *he* would heal and *he* would bring deliverance. It is a sad fact, but some people are ready to follow anyone or anything that appears spiritual. Only God will heal and bring deliverance. And while it is true that He may reveal Himself through humankind, He alone must receive all the glory, praise, and honor.

The flesh attempts to control the moves of God. Many of the things that people label spiritual actually come from the mental realm. You will know whether something is of God or not by discerning whether it points toward or away from self. If someone has a revelation—or even a prophecy—that benefits, exalts, or glorifies self, then it is not from God. The security of the flesh is always centered in another person (self), not in God. *Find your security in God so you will be motivated by commitment rather than by control.*

CHAPTER

5

FIVE

ABUSIVE CONTROL IN THE BIBLE

Now let's examine the problem of abusive control from a biblical perspective. Let's see how Jesus managed to remove Himself from people who sought to abusively control Him:

And when the devil had ended all the temptation, he departed from him for a season. And Jesus returned in the power of the Spirit into Galilee: and there went out a fame of him through all the region round about. And he taught in their synagogues, being glorified of all. And he came to Nazareth, where he had been brought up: and, as his custom was, he went into the synagogue on the sabbath day, and stood up for to read. And there was delivered unto him the book of the prophet Esaias. And when he had opened the book, he found the place where it was written, The Spirit of the Lord is upon me, because he hath anointed me to preach the gospel to the poor; he hath sent me to heal the brokenhearted, to preach deliverance to the captives, and recovering of sight to the blind, to set at liberty them that are bruised, to preach the acceptable year of the Lord. And he closed the book, and he gave it again to the minister, and sat down. And the eyes of all them that were in the synagogue were fastened on him. And he began to say unto them, This day is this scripture fulfilled in your ears. (Luke 4:13–21)

This is an interesting story. Jesus knew His destiny. He knew His call to the earth. But He didn't advertise it before it was time; He kept it to Himself and developed it.

Jesus went through His wilderness experience and won. (See Luke 4:1–13.) Most people go into their wilderness and stay there. They do not get very far when faced with trials and temptation. The first time the devil tells them they can't succeed, they agree. "That's right," they say, and sit down in defeat and despair. God, however, is looking for fighters, not weak-kneed, wishy-washy Christians. The world has seen enough of those people.

> **Jesus went through His wilderness experience and won.**

After Jesus had emerged victorious from His wilderness experience, He walked back to His hometown, Nazareth, the place where He had grown up, and entered the synagogue. This was where His parents had gone to "church." It was where the rabbis had trained Him as a boy. Jesus had learned many good things from the leader of that synagogue. That day, when the rabbi handed the scrolls to Jesus, He opened them and read Isaiah 61:1–2. But Jesus did not read this prophecy as a normal man would read it—as something the people expected to take place in the future. *Jesus read the prophetic message as if it applied to Him—because it did!*

CONTROL IN THE HOME CHURCH

After Jesus had boldly announced, *"This day is this scripture* [prophecy] *fulfilled in your ears"* (Luke 4:21), the people's first reaction was, *"Is not this Joseph's son?"* (verse 22). *The people of Nazareth totally missed the significance of Jesus' declaration that He was the Messiah!* All they could say was, "No, You can't be. You're the son of Joseph, the local carpenter."

As Jesus spoke further, calling Himself a prophet, the people became incensed. (See verses 23–27.)

And all they in the synagogue, when they heard these things, were filled with wrath, and rose up, and thrust him out of the city, and led him unto the brow of the hill whereon their city was built, that they might cast him down headlong. But he passing through the midst of them went his way.

(Luke 4:28–30)

When you take possession of what is yours, spiritually lukewarm people will automatically oppose you! A lukewarm person is double minded. He sits on the fence between listening to his emotions and listening to his spirit.

Jesus closed the book and handed it back to the rabbi. He did the right and respectful thing. He had read forcefully from the Scriptures in the Spirit, but He did not try to take over the meeting. He sat down.

IF LOOKS COULD KILL...

The people of Nazareth were so astonished at Jesus that they did not simply glance at Him; their eyes fastened on Him, as we saw in verse 20. After He had spoken to them strongly about their lack of faith in Him as the promised Messiah (see

Luke 4:23–27), their look became warlike: a look of madness, a look of rage, a look beyond natural understanding—a look that demands to know, "Who do you think you are?" (See verse 28.) Has anyone ever looked at you that way? If you are a true servant of God, you may undergo this type of persecution.

Notice that Jesus did not respond to their anger. And because He didn't, they wanted to destroy Him! This was Jesus, the young man who had grown up in their church. This was Nazareth, one of those small towns where everyone knows everyone else's business! And everyone supposedly loves everyone else, but not now. The people of Nazareth wanted to kill Jesus because He did not withdraw, explain, or falter. He stood His ground. They could not control Him! He was not under their power! When you get to the place where people can't control you through intimidation or other means, they may try to destroy you. They may cast you out. In other words, they may try to excommunicate you.

> **They failed to recognize the Messiah when He was in their midst!**

The people of Nazareth rose up as one to run Jesus out of town and throw Him off a nearby hilltop. (See verse 29.) This was a dramatic excommunication. They wanted to kill Him! This is an example of a controlling spirit that operated through Jesus' home church in an effort to make Him back down from saying that He, the Messiah, had come into the world to fulfill the prophetic Scriptures.

They were looking for God's Anointed One, and they thought they would recognize Him through their usual carnal ways of thinking. But they failed to recognize the Messiah when He came and lived in their midst as one of them! Even after all the teachings He had delivered and all the miracles He had performed among them, they still did not believe that Jesus was the Messiah! Why? Because they had been blinded by *religion*.

What is religion? It is an attempt to know and please God through human effort. *Christianity* is not a religion; it is a relationship with God—walking side by side, talking and communicating with Jesus, the Living Son of God. This personal relationship does not come through religion, in which people seek to know and please God through human artifices and personal opinions.

This is why there are religious spirits—demons sent to bind people from knowing God personally in His fullness. Religious spirits are controlling spirits. They insist on fleshly operations and manifestations to make people feel that they have done a service to God. Religious, controlling spirits hinder the true move of the Spirit of God. They operate through those who walk by the flesh, those who do not know much about life in the Spirit.

Christianity is not a religion; it is a relationship with God.

Such people are very unlearned about a spiritual relationship with Jesus Christ; however, they know all the religious facts, and they usually distort them to control the move of the Holy Spirit.

Notice that in this passage Jesus did not die. He just walked through the midst of that angry crowd and went on His way. He had a destiny to fulfill; humankind could not control Him or abort His mission. Even the ones whom Jesus loved most could not control Him or hinder what God had called Him to do.

THE EARLY CHURCH FACES CONTROL

Now let's turn to the fourth chapter of Acts, where we will see an example of attempted control in the early church. We will see how the religious leaders of Israel attempted to control the apostles Peter and John after the lame man at the Gate Beautiful had been healed through them by the power of Jesus' name:

> *And as* [Peter and John] *spake unto the people, the priests, and the captain of the temple, and the Sadducees, came upon them, being grieved that they taught the people, and preached through Jesus the resurrection from the dead. And they laid hands on them, and put them in hold unto the next day: for it was now eventide....And it came to pass on the morrow, that their rulers, and elders, and scribes, and Annas the high priest, and Caiaphas, and John, and Alexander, and as many as were of the kindred of the high priest, were gathered together at Jerusalem. And when they had set them in the midst, they asked, By what power, or by what name, have ye done this? Then Peter, filled with the Holy Ghost, said unto them, Ye rulers of the people, and elders of Israel, If we this day be examined of the good deed done to the impotent man, by what means he is made whole; Be it known unto you all* [not just some of you, *all* of you], *and to all the people of Israel, that by the name of Jesus Christ of Nazareth, whom ye crucified, whom God raised from the dead, even by him doth this man stand here before you whole.* (Acts 4:1–3, 5–10)

That was a bold statement. Here, all the religious spirits in town had come together to attack Peter and John for healing a sick man! This tells us that religious spirits are not on the side

44

of God because healing a sick person should anger no one. Instead, there should be rejoicing!

Have you noticed from this Scripture passage that people who are religious have no common sense? They think they are on fire for God, but in reality they are very cold spiritually. When someone tells them that they are cold spiritually, or when God uses someone outside of their control system, they become very angry!

CONTROLLING PEOPLE AND RELIGIOUS PEOPLE

There is really no way to separate controlling people from religious people. Controlling spirits and religious spirits are alike. They are twins. It is hard to have one without the other. You will find many controllers among those who are very religious, but notice that Peter was not afraid to respond to strong religious people. One way to stand up to controlling, religious spirits is never to fear them and always to have a spiritual response ready to give to them. Also notice that when abusive controllers began to attack God's servants, a response to them was always recorded in the Bible.

> **You must state the truth when you confront a controlling person.**

Why were the religious leaders of Jerusalem attacking the apostles? To stop them from healing the people in the name of Jesus. The leaders were afraid that the healings would affect their control over people whom they thought they owned. Peter, being full of the Holy Spirit, explained to all of these religious leaders that healing people is a good deed (see Acts 4:9), not a wicked or mischievous deed. When confronting controlling people, you need to state the truth. Don't just suggest it; state it. That's what Peter did. He went on to tell the leaders that the healing had come about *"by the name of Jesus Christ of Nazareth, whom ye crucified"* (Acts 4:10). That is another bold statement!

Peter was addressing the same leaders who had allowed a murderer to go free in order to have Jesus crucified. Peter's bold statements didn't make these controlling, religious people very happy. They marveled at the apostles, but they also made degrading statements about them:

> *Now when they saw the boldness of Peter and John, and perceived that they were unlearned and ignorant men, they marvelled; and they took knowledge of them, that they had been with Jesus. And beholding the man which was healed standing with them, they could say nothing against it. But when they had commanded them* [which is characteristic of controllers; they don't ask, they command. There is always an undercurrent of demand in their statements, causing the other person to feel obligated to comply with their desires.] *to go aside out of the council, they conferred among themselves, saying, What shall we do to these men? for that indeed a notable miracle hath been done by them is manifest to all them that dwell in Jerusalem; and we cannot deny it. But that it spread no further among the people, let us straitly threaten them, that they speak henceforth to no man in this name. And they called them, and commanded them not to speak at all nor teach in the name of Jesus.* (Acts 4:13–18)

BIBLICAL THREATS

We have discussed the abusive threats that can manifest in daily living. But now let's see the biblical threats that the men of God had to deal with in the Scriptures.

Notice the phrase in verse 17, *"let us straitly **threaten** them"* (emphasis added). What does a threat do to a person? It makes him go against what he believes; it forces him to submit to those who are intimidating him. That is abusive control! The religious leaders of that day threatened the apostles by commanding *"them not to speak at all or teach at all in the name of Jesus"* (verse 18 NASB). That was control, and the apostles had a decision to make in response to it.

How did Peter and John react in the face of these threats and demands?

> *But Peter and John answered and said unto them, Whether it be right in the sight of God to hearken unto you more than unto God, judge ye. For we cannot but speak the things which we have seen and heard. So when they had **further threatened them**, they let them go, finding nothing how they might punish them, because of the people: for all men glorified God for that which was done.*
>
> (Acts 4:19–21, emphasis added)

I like these apostles! They stood their ground before all the religious spirits in town. The religious leaders were angry because a miracle had been done—and because it hadn't been done through them! They thought *they* should have been the ones to perform the miracle because they were the religious rulers.

God is looking for human beings who will be obedient to His Spirit.

However, God could not use them because they were full of pride, thinking they knew it all.

God is not looking for a person who operates from his head, by his own way of thinking. God is looking for someone who operates from his heart, by his spirit. God is looking for human beings who will be obedient to His Spirit.

That is why it bothers some well-educated, prideful people when God uses someone who has little or no formal education to be a miracle worker. People who are filled with pride usually criticize those who have nothing in the natural. But how can God use those who are relying on their education alone? The *only* way an education works for a person is by *submitting it to the will of God* and not relying upon it but solely upon God!

In the seventh verse of Acts 4, these religious leaders asked the apostles, *"By what power, or by what name, have ye done this?"* They were saying, "Who do you think you are, doing such a thing without our permission? By whose authority did you do this?"

BIBLICAL DEFEAT OF CONTROL

The eighth verse continues, *"Then Peter, filled with the Holy Ghost, said unto them."*

The only way to win over control is to be full of the Holy Spirit and power! Just like Peter, we need the Spirit of might in order to win over the spirits of control. Though it is important to speak words of faith and not of doubt, the Spirit of might (see Isaiah 11:2) does not come upon a person as a result of his reciting positive confessions or following prescribed formulas. It will not stay on an individual just because he associates with the right people.

The Spirit of might places a passion within the believer that will motivate him to hate evil and will empower him to carry out God's plan in the earth. The Spirit of might resides as a nuclear force within the individual who propels him forward over every evil opponent that may attempt to restrain him. The Spirit of might confronts resistance. It provides the individual the ability to distinguish right from wrong in any situation and to go on from there. It never defends; it simply endows the person it indwells with the power to state the facts!

The Spirit of might gives the human mind the supernatural ability to remain in peace and to rest in the midst of battle. It brings the assurance of the coming victory and causes the joy of the Lord to manifest around the one who possesses it.

> **The Spirit of might gives victory over every evil opponent.**

The Spirit of might also endows the physical body and the emotions with endurance and protection. It supplies the supernatural ability to carry on far beyond the natural, soulish limitations. The Spirit of might never comes upon a person for the purpose of self-gain. It comes in order that the purpose of God may be fulfilled in the earth through the church!

Peter had the Spirit of might in and upon him as he spoke to the religious leaders of his day. In Acts 4:10, he continued his discourse by telling them, "By the name of Jesus Christ of Nazareth—whom you crucified—that's by whose name we performed this miracle, and by whose name we will continue to perform miracles!" The religious leaders responded by commanding the apostles to stop teaching and preaching in this name, threatening them severely if they did not obey.

But what did Peter and John do? They went back to their own company and told everyone of the things that had happened. (See verse 23.) Did the church in the book of Acts shrink back because of the report they received from the apostles? No! The Spirit of might came on all of them! (See Acts 4:31.) Instead of hiding in their homes and asking God to slay their enemies, they got down on their faces and asked the Lord to grant them more boldness that they might *"speak thy word, by stretching forth thine hand to heal; and that signs and wonders* [might] *be done by the name of thy holy child Jesus"* (Acts 4:29–30).

Their response and request so pleased the Lord that He shook the place where they assembled and filled them with the boldness of the Holy Spirit! (See verse 31.) He united them with one heart and one purpose, and none of them lacked anything. (See verses 32–33.)

And much to the horror of the religious, controlling leaders of that day, God gave great power to those who believed. (See verse 33.) That meant that more healings, more deliverances, and more salvation experiences took place in the city of Jerusalem after Peter and John had been threatened than ever before!

Let this be our testimony today. Ask God to fill you with the Spirit of might so that you may blast through abusive, controlling spirits and then fulfill the plan and purpose of God in the earth!

CHAPTER

6

SIX

POSITIVE, JUSTIFIABLE CONTROL

Just as we have discussed the negative aspects of control, we need to study its positive nature as well. God has ordained a good and justifiable control for our well-being. If it is God's and we submit to it, positive control will groom us and shape us into maturity.

Moderation characterizes justifiable control, along with good, sensible regulations and restraints that bring excitement without the abuse of personal rights. For example, the United States government has many controls that help protect the well-being and enhance the happiness of the American people. Some of these include 1) drug laws, 2) immigration controls, and 3) federal regulations covering such vital matters as protection of public health, food inspection, conservation of natural resources, provision for education, and so forth.

If we do not allow ourselves to be controlled by proper moderation, regulations, and restraints, we will have problems with excesses. Positive, justifiable control serves as a godly balance in our lives.

We have a responsibility to God to follow mature, seasoned leadership. We are to be submitted to such leaders, to heed their wise counsel according to the Word of God. The greatest Teacher of all, the Holy Spirit, can reveal to us the attributes to look for in those who exercise godly, positive control.

THE HOLY SPIRIT

The Holy Spirit is still present on the earth today. His example in our lives should be the standard by which we pattern our relationships with others.

The Holy Spirit is the controller of the life of the believer. The Holy Spirit is not a dictator. He does not push us, pressure us, or smother our creativity. He is the perfect balance. The Holy Spirit will convict us of sin in our lives so we can be cleansed and go on with the plan of God unhindered. He will not condemn us, harass us, beat us down, or torment us, no matter how grievous our mistakes might be. God does not come to crush us but to make us whole. His purpose is not to place us in bondage but to set us free. The Holy Spirit gives us the freedom to express God through our own individual personalities.

> **God does not come to crush us but to make us whole.**

The Lord does not make our choices for us, nor does He harshly demand obedience from us. He does correct us, but to obey is always our choice. In John 16:13, Jesus said, *"Howbeit when he, the Spirit of truth, is come, he will guide you into all truth."*

The Holy Spirit came to guide us into the truth of the gospel. That is true and responsible leadership. He serves as a conductor of the revelation of God in our lives. Notice that He will guide us, but following His guidance is our responsibility.

The next part of that same verse highlights another characteristic of true, godly leadership: *"For he shall not speak of himself; but whatsoever he shall hear, that shall he speak: and he will show you things to come."*

The Holy Spirit never points to Himself. He never exalts Himself or attempts to promote Himself. He never competes to be seen or heard. He speaks to us only what He hears from the Father, and if we will listen to Him and trust Him, He will tell us of things to come.

The first part of Romans 8:26 tells us more about the Holy Spirit and about good, positive control in our lives: *"Likewise the Spirit also **helpeth** our infirmities* [weaknesses]."

The Holy Spirit "helps" us. He will not do the job for us, neither will He expend all the effort needed to accomplish the task at hand. He will help us to fulfill the plan and purpose of God on the earth. A minister friend of mine once put it this way: "The Holy Spirit will help you do a job, just as I would help you move a chair. You pick up one side of the chair, and I lift the

> **The Holy Spirit will not do the job for us, but He helps us to fulfill it.**

other. That is how the Holy Spirit helps the believer."

Positive control will never pressure, condemn, or smother. It will love and provide the encouragement needed to live life to the fullest for God. Positive control serves as a safety valve, a "check and balance," for your daily walk. Positive control exercised through a person helps and guides, but this kind of control does not do so for self-gain. Positive control gives an individual the freedom, within the boundaries of the Word of

God, to be himself and to express his own individual personality and creativity.

POSITIVE CONTROL THROUGH LEADERSHIP

It is imperative that we understand one important principle: God has always appointed leaders, and spiritual leaders must exercise legitimate, godly authority. Let's begin our study of this vital principle in Ephesians 4:11–14. I like the way The *Amplified Bible* translates this passage:

> *And His gifts were [varied; He Himself appointed and gave men to us] some to be apostles (special messengers), some prophets (inspired preachers and expounders), some evangelists (preachers of the Gospel, traveling missionaries), some pastors (shepherds of His flock) and teachers. His intention was the **perfecting** and the **full equipping** of the saints (His consecrated people), [that they should do] the work of ministering toward building up Christ's body (the church), [that it might develop] until we all attain oneness in the faith and in the comprehension of the [full and accurate] knowledge of the Son of God, that [we might arrive] at really mature manhood (the completeness of personality which is nothing less than the standard height of Christ's own perfection), the measure of the stature of the fullness of the Christ and the completeness found in Him. So then, we may no longer be children, tossed [like ships] to and fro between chance gusts of teaching and wavering with every changing wind of doctrine, [the prey of] the cunning and cleverness of unscrupulous men, [gamblers engaged] in every shifting form of trickery in inventing errors to mislead.* (emphasis added)

Notice that it was the intention of the Lord to give certain leadership gifts to men and women to help the body of

Christ come into maturity and to know Him in an intimate way. These leadership gifts are often referred to as the fivefold ministry.

These leaders are given gifts to help "equip" and "perfect" the believers. In Strong's concordance, the Greek word translated *perfecting* in this verse is derived from a root word meaning to "fit, mend, prepare, restore."[1] *Fit, mend, prepare, restore:* These small words spell hard work and discipline. The job of the fivefold ministry is to see to it that you and I are thoroughly endowed with faith, love, and hope, and fully equipped with the comprehension of the Son of God, the works and sensitivity of the Holy Spirit, and the knowledge of every other aspect of the Word of God. God holds them accountable to Him for their leadership over us. God, in turn, holds us accountable for the degree of our submissiveness to that leadership.

Please understand that God holds you and me accountable to the leadership—the *office* and the *gifts* of the leaders, not the leaders themselves. We are to follow them as they follow the Word of God. When people in leadership positions accurately demonstrate the Scriptures, God holds us accountable for how we submit to the gift inside of them.

The *Amplified Bible* version of Hebrews 13:17 reads,

Obey your spiritual leaders and submit to them [continually recognizing their authority over you], for they are constantly keeping watch over your souls and guarding your spiritual welfare, as men who will have to render an account [of their trust]. [Do your part to] let them do this with gladness

---

[1] James Strong, *Strong's Exhaustive Concordance of the Bible* (Nashville: Abingdon, 1890) "Hebrew and Chaldee Dictionary," p. 40, G#2677.

and not with sighing and groaning, for that would not be profitable to you [either].

In order for a leader to fit, mend, prepare, and restore us, he must have some degree of positive, justifiable control over our lives. Refusal to submit to such protection and wisdom would mean outright rebellion on the part of the believer.

Because the body of Christ has been vague on this issue, whenever strong leadership has surfaced, the people have scattered, shouting, "Control! Control!" Let us, as believers, grow up and become mature. We need strong leadership in this decade. The world does not hint at or suggest sin any longer. The world is blatant in its extremity. We, as the people of God, need to stand behind the strong leadership that God is raising up in our midst. We must follow these people as our examples in fulfilling the plan and purpose of heaven.

> **Leadership is positive action— not just talk, but actually doing something.**

The church must "shake" two attitudes: 1) compromise on the part of its leaders; and 2) despising of and rebellion against strong leadership on the part of the people.

Leadership is positive action. It is not just talking; it is actually doing something. It is moving forward with the Lord and taking the people along as it goes. If leadership is not strong today, the body of Christ will not grow to full maturity tomorrow.

As I was studying this subject, I was told that, when the modern Israeli army goes into battle, its officers are sent in first; then the troops follow. This is said to be one of the reasons why the Israelis are so militarily successful: Their officers move out front, showing the troops which way to go and what to do. Other nations send their troops in first, while their leaders sit well behind the lines, viewing the battle through binoculars.

That is what some church leaders do today: They try to lead by remaining in the background. Part of this situation is the fault of the people because they do not understand good, godly, justifiable control. Whenever those in positions of leadership attempt to fit, mend, prepare, or restore lives, the people develop a rebellious attitude and label the leadership as controlling.

Remember that leaders are people too. They are human beings with real emotions and feelings just like everyone else. When their churches continuously label and betray them, they have a tendency to withdraw for protection against further hurts, wounds, and slander. If God has blessed you with a strong leader, then follow that leader as he or she follows Christ.

If we are to be spiritually mature, we must receive, submit, and grow.

Godly leadership will rise to the occasion and take the lead. When God speaks to leaders and tells their local body or nation to step out in an area of faith, they boldly take action. Those believers who are sensitive to the Spirit of God will follow and support the cause with all their hearts.

Positive, justifiable control will confront the issues that are contrary to the purpose of God! Many times when the Spirit of the Lord causes people to "step out," there will also be an extra grooming of their character, integrity, and faith. The job of the leader is to instruct and discipline according to the Word of God. If you and I are to go on to full spiritual maturity, we must receive, submit, and grow. We must be willing to face the reality of where we stand spiritually and then move on into maturity.

Leaders must not be afraid to confront any disorderly conduct that might take place in their services. I am a strong believer in prayer and intercession, but many times some of the intercessors are filled with a confused sense of worth and begin to think they are the most spiritual people in the church. Some have even tried to use their positions to control the pastor or other leaders.

Every believer is called to the ministry of intercession. The reason some seem to be more anointed than others in the area of prayer is because they use it more! There is no scriptural reference to an office of intercessor. An intercessor is a servant of God who is sensitive to His leadings to pray His will into the earth. An intercessor paves the way for the Holy Spirit to disarrange and thwart the schemes of the enemy. Prayers of intercession make the plan of God a reality for the hour.

Every believer is called to the ministry of intercession.

Intercessors must be instructed in the spirit realm and in the Word of God in order to pray accurately in the will of God. Believers must be instructed in the ways and the character of God if they are to hear Him clearly. That is not abusive control! That is the positive control of the fivefold ministry. Pastors must not be afraid to confront intercessors who are in error. They must not be hesitant to instruct them to pray decently and in order or else quit interceding in public worship until they can behave normally as they should.

I like leaders who are not afraid to confront and correct misdoing! That kind of godly boldness shows me that they value the presence of the Holy Spirit in their midst. Such a positive confrontation reveals that the leader is committed to the maturity of the body of Christ so that the world will be motivated to hunger for what we believers have. In strong leadership there is security for the people of God. There is hope for the world through God's strong leaders and believers!

Religious, rebellious spirits do not like strong leadership! Such spirits want to dominate and control a church and its people. If you have been confronted by a spiritual leader who has suggested that a change needs to take place in your personal life, rejoice and thank God for that individual!

Yes, the searing light of the Holy Spirit hurts our flesh at times, but it is for our own good. Our spiritual growth and maturity depend on it. As the body of Christ, we are in training, so we must expect to be groomed and changed! Countless others await the benefit from the training experience through which you and I will be successfully brought to full maturity.

Strong, positive control from a leader is an indication of his or her commitment to God. Do not rob yourself of the protection that God has ordained through those He has set in leadership positions in His church. We are an army, and in order to war effectively and triumphantly, we must be united in purpose and fervency. We must not break rank in order to pamper our own soulish desires.

Do not shrink back from godly leaders who have given their lives for your benefit and maturity. Be thankful for godly direction in your life. What you learn from it will be your dearest treasure on the battlefield.

CHAPTER

SEVEN

POSITIVE, BIBLICAL CONTROL

L et's look at a biblical story concerning strong leadership and a rebellious spirit that tried to prevail against it.

THE LEADERSHIP OF MOSES

We find a very interesting situation in Numbers 16. In the camp of the Israelites, there arose a man named Korah, a descendant of Levi, who went among the tribes complaining about the leadership of Moses. He thought Moses had taken too much power and authority upon himself as leader of God's people. In other words, Korah thought Moses was a controller.

When Korah had secured enough backing from other disgruntled children of Israel, he and his followers approached Moses, God's chosen leader. In studying verse 2 of this passage, I find very interesting the type of people Korah recruited to join his cause:

And they rose up before Moses, with certain of the children of Israel, two hundred and fifty princes of the assembly, famous in the congregation, men of renown.

(Number 16:2)

Korah did not have God behind him, so he had to recruit the most famous men among the tribes of Israel in an attempt to give himself validity.

When these dissenters—including many of the other Levites who served in the temple worship—had assembled together, they approached Moses and Aaron. There Korah presented his accusation against these men of God:

Ye take too much upon you, seeing all the congregation are holy, every one of them, and the LORD is among them: wherefore then lift ye up yourselves above the congregation of the LORD? And when Moses heard it, he fell upon his face. (Numbers 16:3–4)

Do these words sound familiar? "You are taking too much upon yourself, because everyone in this church is as holy as you are. Why are you lifting yourself up before the people? We can hear from God just as well as you can!"

These Israelites did not recognize the divine, positive control that had been given to Moses and Aaron by God Himself. Instead jealousy drove them. They were motivated by their desire for power and blinded to the truth by religion and rebellion.

In order to walk in the fullness of divine leadership, a heavy price must be paid. If not for the grace of God, the weight of it at times would be almost unbearable. The main price that must be paid by a leader concerns the daily life he or she must lead before the people. To walk in the fullness of divine authority—to exercise justifiable control—the leader must live in a certain way. Divine leaders must pursue the way of righteousness and holiness. They must have a strong desire for God and hate evil with all of their hearts.

The devil wants to control the human will. If he can control a person's will, he can control the person. Compromise will weaken an individual's ability to take a strong stand against Satan. When you and I are strong and refuse to bow to evil and wrong, some will try to find something wrong with us in order to destroy our character, undermine our stand, and overcome our strength. But divine leaders must pay the price of faithfulness, no matter what comes against them—a price that causes heaven to take notice. God will move the foundations of the earth for the faithful.

Divine leaders must pursue the way of righteousness and holiness.

Divine leaders must walk in accuracy and discernment in the Spirit. They will not change their stand just because they are under attack from the enemy. They will continue to obey God in the midst of conflict and adversity.

After Moses had heard the accusation levied against him and Aaron by Korah and his followers, he fell on his face before the Lord. Then he rose up to speak to Korah and the sons of Levi who were with him:

> *Seemeth it but a small thing unto you, that the God of Israel hath separated you from the congregation of Israel, to bring you near to himself to do the service of the tabernacle of the* Lord, *and to stand before the congregation to minister unto them? And he hath brought thee near to him, and all thy brethren the sons of Levi with thee: and seek ye the priesthood also?* (Numbers 16:9–10)

What Moses was asking them was simply this: "Is it nothing to you that the Lord has chosen you to stand in His house and minister to Him before the people? Do you see your place in the body as such a minor thing? And having (obviously) failed at that, do you actually think you have paid the price to stand in the office of the priesthood?"

When Korah and the Levites refused to listen to the reasoning of Moses, the man of God proclaimed, "Tomorrow the Lord will show who is His chosen leader." (See Numbers 16:5.)

God will never forsake the godly leaders He has ordained.

After Moses had gone before the Lord, God instructed him to have the people choose the side they were on: Korah's or Moses'. After the children of Israel had run to whichever side they had chosen, Moses stood before them and declared,

Hereby ye shall know that the LORD hath sent me to do all these works; for I have not done them of mine own mind.
(Numbers 16:28)

He continued to speak, warning the people that if the Lord was on his side, the earth would open up and swallow the rebellious Korah and his group because they had provoked the Lord their God. The Bible records that as soon as Moses had finished speaking, the earth did open up and swallow Korah, his family, and all his goods; so they vanished from the congregation. God then sent a fire to consume the two hundred and fifty murmurers who had gathered with Korah. (See verses 30–35.)

God will never forsake the godly leaders He has ordained, no matter who or what should rise up against them. Moses continually showed his heart for the people in the face of God. He confronted the people with bold leadership in order to turn them back to the Lord.

THE LEADERSHIP OF PAUL

The ministry of the apostle Paul gives us another example of positive, biblical control in the area of leadership.

Paul made a very bold statement to the Corinthians:

For though ye have ten thousand instructors in Christ, yet have ye not many fathers: for in Christ Jesus I have begotten you through the gospel. Wherefore I beseech you, be ye followers of me. (1 Corinthians 4:15–16)

Look at the security Paul enjoyed in his position as a leader! He told the church in Corinth, which he had established, "Even though you have heard many teachers and preachers, I am the one who led you to spiritual birth. Therefore, follow my example and lifestyle."

How many of us would say that Paul practiced abusive control? None of us! Yet I dare say that if a leader today should make such a bold statement as this one by Paul, many would have him labeled before the sun came up!

Again, look at what Paul said in his letter to the church in Philippi: *"Brethren, be followers together of me, and mark them which walk so as ye have us for an ensample"* (Philippians 3:17).

Not only did Paul tell the Philippian believers to follow his lifestyle, he also said that they should watch those who followed him, for they were good examples of Christianity. That shows secure leadership!

As a leader chosen and anointed by God, Paul took his responsibility seriously. He watched carefully over the flock of believers under his authority, and many times he wrote to them, "Although I am not there with you in the flesh, know that I am with you in spirit." Second Corinthians 11:2 reveals the intensity with which Paul related to his flock:

> *For I am jealous over you with godly jealousy: for I have espoused you to one husband, that I may present you as a chaste virgin to Christ.*

As a leader, Paul was jealous over those he had brought to Jesus. He was constantly on guard against anyone or anything that might come to steal the people of God away from their first love, Jesus Christ. He fought against the sin that might blemish the church. He did not hesitate to confront because of the love he had for Jesus. He wanted everyone who believed to come into the full maturity that the resurrection had provided for them. He took the risk of being hated, persecuted, and killed so that lives could be saved. That's not abusive control—that shows positive, justifiable, godly leadership!

Paul never desired or sought for men to exalt him. He was a true servant of God. In Galatians 1, I believe he revealed his true heart as he gave the account of his salvation and training experience. He had done great works for the Lord, but as he finished relating the story, he said this of the people who had heard him speak: *"And they glorified God in me"* (Galatians 1:24, emphasis added).

The whole key to positive, biblical control is that no matter how many decisions we make, how many conversions we produce, how many people are healed or delivered by our message, or how many foes we conquer, our primary concern is that Jesus Christ be seen first and foremost in every situation we face.

CHAPTER

EIGHT

ARE YOU A CONTROLLER?

We have learned the attributes of negative, abusive control; positive, justifiable control; and positive, biblical control. Since we now have this understanding, it is important to rid ourselves of any tendencies we may have in the negative areas. Learning these things about control will cause some of us to think immediately of people we know who are controllers.

But what if you suspect that you may have a controlling personality? How can you recognize whether you have a tendency to be an abusive controller?

1. **You have a tendency to be an abusive controller if you feel that the only way you can be important or accepted is by giving orders and making demands.**

Do not allow ambition and desire for power to drive you. Ambition and power seeking will not produce godly authority. In Matthew 8, Jesus marveled at the humility of a Roman centurion. Beginning in verse 8, we read this exchange between Jesus and this military leader:

The centurion answered and said, Lord, I am not worthy that thou shouldest come under my roof: but speak the word only, and my servant shall be healed. For I am a man under authority, having soldiers under me: and I say to this man, Go, and he goeth; and to another, Come, and he cometh; and to my servant, Do this, and he doeth it.

(Matthew 8:8–9)

Jesus replied that He had not found such faith in all of Israel. (See verse 10.) This man had learned the principle of godly leadership and authority. In his humility to those in authority over him, he had become an authority himself. He was a trusted leader, one whose commands could be followed and fulfilled.

> **When we submit ourselves to God, He will lift us up in due season.**

When we submit ourselves to God, He will lift us up in due season. When that season comes, our sense of worth will come from a trust in Him, not from our ability to give orders or commands.

2. **You have a tendency to be an abusive controller if you feel possessive about a person or persons, if you feel that others have to "check in" with you because you know more than they do or what is best for them, if you never accept their judgment of what they think they should do, or if you always belittle them because you are convinced they don't know anything.**

Possessive people always try to make others feel that they don't know anything, that they are totally ignorant and immature. Possessive controllers make others feel that the only way they are going to survive is by consulting with themselves and doing what they say. When anyone voices an opinion to controllers, they cut that individual down by saying, "Oh, that isn't true. You're wrong; I'm right." One sure sign that you are an abusive controller is if you never allow any differing opinions or ideas to be discussed, accepted, or even expressed. The other person's voice goes in one ear and out the other while you continue to "do your own thing."

3. **You have a tendency to be an abusive controller if you begin to feel intense jealousy over another person, especially if that jealousy dominates your opinions and actions.**

For example, if the person you have been controlling starts talking to someone else, you will automatically feel jealous, possessive, and threatened, and you will probably try to cut off that relationship. You will intrude into the conversation in order to monitor it!

4. **You have a tendency to be an abusive controller if you feel threatened by another person's new relationship.**

You are a controller if you feel that your friendship and relationship with another person are threatened if he or she speaks to someone else, prays with another individual, goes out to dinner with somebody besides you, or engages in any other activity with anyone but you, even for as little as five minutes.

Remember, commitment isn't control!

I limit this discussion to people in friendship relationships, not to people in marriages. A married person's best friend should be his or her mate. A married couple has made a commitment to each other in the sight of God and man. Marriage implies a certain amount of exclusiveness. We will discuss this issue in a later chapter.

5.   You have a tendency to be an abusive controller if you feel that you must protect the other person from every experience.

Let's discuss this topic in more detail. If you feel that you must shield a person from life's experiences, then you are guilty of carrying his or her responsibilities. Every individual must give account for his own behavior. But, a controller attempts to shield another from personal responsibility, often then turning around and getting angry with the other person for not being more responsible. The controller then feels used, cheated, and abused.

This kind of overprotection can happen in any relationship, especially between a parent and child. When an individual has reached maturity, protecting him or her from life's experiences is a destructive form of helping. The Bible says that godly wisdom and understanding come from God's Word and life's experiences. (See Proverbs 3:13 AMP.) Experiences, both good and bad, groom our characters and cause us to walk in the wisdom of God. The varied experiences of life, coupled with the Word of God, season us and bring us understanding.

> **The experiences of life groom our characters and bring us understanding.**

An abusive controller is one who tries to "fix" people's feelings, do their thinking for them, or solve their problems for them. If you shield someone else from experiences he has chosen, then no character is formed in that individual. It will be a never-ending cycle of protection. Both of you will end up feeling frustrated and abused.

I am not talking about a genuine act of love and respect. I am speaking of an unnatural drive to take responsibility for someone else. This behavior is actually an insult to the other person. The abusive controller is making a statement that the other individual is incompetent and incapable of making a choice or decision for himself.

In such cases, usually the other person has never asked the controller for help. That is why the controller gets angry when the other person goes on his way, seemingly ungrateful. Most abusive controllers truly believe they are helping others when they shield them from experiences. They may even think it is cruel or heartless to let others face up to their own dilemmas. Many controllers even twist and control the Scriptures on love and giving as they relate to abusive control. But the Word of God should set us free—not hold us in bondage.

Jesus held people accountable for fulfilling their own responsibilities. Notice throughout the Gospels how Jesus Himself reacted to those who came to Him seeking healing, deliverance, or some other miracle. He always responded to the needs of people by asking them a question—for He knew that the answer they gave would reveal the true nature of their hearts.

Each of us must go through our own experiences in life. But we are not helpless! Jesus Christ has given us a gift—the resurrection power of the Holy Spirit living inside of us. And that's not all. The power of His Spirit within will guide us into truth and victory!

You must also understand that a controlling person thinks and talks about the other individual all the time. If anything keeps the other person from spending time with the controller, the controller will attack that thing and attempt to get rid of it as quickly as possible. He will go to any length or any expense to make sure the person he is controlling spends the majority of his or her time with him.

This is *domination!*

The controlling person will dominate the other individual's vacations, dates, marriage, job, home buying, church going, or even personal finances. An abusive controller will dominate every area of another's life if allowed to do so. If the other person is not careful, he or she can become so entwined with a controller that, in extreme cases, it will take years to get free of that relationship.

6.   **You have a tendency to be an abusive controller if you react in an unnatural way to statements made about the person you are controlling.**

For example, if someone makes a positive statement about the person you control, you will automatically criticize the controlled person to make sure that no friendship develops between them. On the other hand, if someone makes a negative statement about you, the controller, you will immediately defend yourself with a positive statement to make yourself look good.

7.   **You have a tendency to be an abusive controller if you attempt to overprotect—even to the point of hindering God's Spirit.**

For example, sometimes elders or deacons can be so protective of the church that they won't allow the pastor to flow under the anointing of the Lord; they won't help him do what God has told him to do.

Individually, an abusive controller can be so protective of another person that he will not allow that individual to venture out and experience God for himself or herself. The abusive controller is afraid that the person being controlled will make a mistake. Therefore, fear motivates at the core of every decision. *Because fear is the motive* in overprotection, positive growth, whether individual or corporate, is hindered.

8. **You have a tendency to be an abusive controller if you make plans for the other person without his or her permission.**

An abusive controller actually makes plans for the other person without even asking permission to do so! If the individual who is being controlled doesn't want to follow the plan, he is usually made to feel so guilty that he ends up going along with it anyway. He knows that if he doesn't agree, all hell will break loose!

Has a relative ever volunteered your services on a certain project without your permission? You knew that if you didn't agree, they would wage a war in the family for weeks. That's control. Many families are so controlled that they never enjoy a normal life.

God did not design human beings to live miserable lives under other people's control, following other people's plans and designs for their lives. He meant each person to live his or her own life with Him. If anyone thinks he has a right to control another person's life in order to assure his or her success, he believes a lie!

9. **You have a tendency to be an abusive controller if you think the person you control owes you something, and you demand that it be paid back.**

Here is an example of this kind of control. A mom and dad have a boy, Rick, who has been a very good son. He hasn't been rebellious in any way. He feels a call to the ministry. But because he enters Bible school or seminary instead of engineering school, his parents have a fit! They want him to have "security" in life. They nag, cry, interfere, and generally do everything they can to get Rick to change his mind, leave school, return to his hometown, and enroll at the local state university. (They also want him to live at home, of course, so they can continue to supervise him.) They stress their belief that he owes them this consideration because they are his parents and have devoted their lives to rearing him.

This is a perfect example of control versus call.

Such people fail to see that the call of God on an individual's life is the highest calling in life! There is a way to biblically honor one's parents and still go on with God. He is the One who must be answered to. Rick must follow Elisha's advice, respectfully kiss his parents good-bye, and follow God. (See 1 Kings 19:20.) The Lord will take care of the rest.

God is the One who must be answered to.

If you and I do our best to be obedient to the call of God upon our lives, everything else will eventually fall into place. Learn to trust God.

10. You have a tendency to be an abusive controller if you try to manipulate people through use of flattery.

Actually, if you are a controller, you can go to the extreme in either direction. You can cut others down so low with your words that they feel that if they don't do what you say, you might write "infidel" across their foreheads. Or you can use honeyed words to flatter people into complying with your wishes and desires.

This is the way some ministries grow. The preacher not only controls his people through flattery, he also gets money out of them by the same means! He pumps them up by telling them how much he and God love them. Yet such people won't help the girl who has had an abortion. They won't minister to those plagued with AIDS. They don't want mixed nationalities or races in their congregations. They refuse to receive certain types of people in their churches because it doesn't look nice.

Ministers have to be careful not to flatter one another for the purpose of getting the speakers and support they desire and need. We must never forget that only God exalts and only God brings down.

In the *Amplified Bible* version, Daniel 11:32 states of the Antichrist, *"And such as violate the covenant he shall pervert and seduce with flatteries."*

> **We must not forget that only God exalts and only God brings down.**

We have a covenant with God regarding the plan and destiny for our lives. Those who do not recognize God as their sole Source and Security will fall victim to flattery. But the good news is that this verse goes on!

But the people who know their God shall prove themselves strong and shall stand firm and do exploits [for God].

Whether as a believer or a leader, your personal security should depend on God, and God alone. Being secure in the Lord will enhance your other relationships. A ministry will never grow unless God is the security, foundation, and source of it. We must lie down with our faces bowed before God and cry out to Him. We must not be afraid to go before the Lord and give Him our troubles and cares. In return, He will fill us with His strength. Giving our all to God means just that: turning over to Him every part of us, and then leaving it there with Him, trusting Him to handle it for us. *"Faithful is he that calleth you, who also will do it"* (1 Thessalonians 5:24).

That is why we give ourselves to God. "Self" cannot be our source or our comfort. That is why we say, "It is not some of self and some of God; *it is none of self and all of God."*

CHAPTER

9
NINE

CONTROL BY PARENTS

In the next three chapters, we will discuss the main "hot spots" of control. We will examine the negative and the positive aspects of control in these vital areas.

As we have seen, controlling spirits most often attempt to work through the people nearest us—even family members—rather than through strangers. We must be careful that the normal control in a family situation—such as the natural control that the Bible indicates a parent is to exercise over a child—does not become unnatural or abusive. Adults in a family can consciously or unconsciously limit a young person's ability to succeed in life. This happens because of negative, fearful, or unscriptural family attitudes or customs.

In Ezekiel 18:2–24, God told Ezekiel that He looks at families as individuals.

What mean ye, that ye use this proverb concerning the land of Israel, saying, The fathers have eaten sour grapes, and the children's teeth are set on edge? As I live, saith the Lord GOD, ye shall not have occasion any more to use this proverb in Israel. (Ezekiel 18:2–3)

God didn't want Ezekiel or the Israelites to say that a person is bound by what their parents or grandparents did. God wants us to know we have freedom from the past, and we are free now to obey Him. Letting genealogy dictate our lives can place on us boundaries of limitations inherited from family members or handed down through family philosophy and tradition, boundaries God never intended to limit us. Many times a response or reaction comes from a motive shadowed by spirits of poverty, fear, or bitterness. These motivating spirits in a family will cause an abusive control to dominate it, sometimes for generations. In order to succeed in the fullness that God has for each of us, we must break these controlling spirits and nullify their effects upon us.

The first step to doing that is to realize that, in God's eyes, these bondages to the past do not hold us. We are free in Jesus to obey and to live the abundant life. He doesn't just say to Ezekiel that we are free. He says that we shall live, and He means to live the abundant life. In the New Testament, Jesus says the same thing in His hometown when He pro-

> **We are free in Jesus to obey and to live the abundant life.**

claims through Isaiah that He has come to set captives free. (See Luke 4:18–21.) God does not want families to be under the domination of the past through these spirits any longer.

Some examples of the responses motivated by such controlling spirits are:

1. "No one in this family may ever buy a new car, only a used one."

2. "No one in this family will ever leave our church or denomination because our grandfather helped establish it."

3. "No one in this family may marry without the approval of the other family members; no one is allowed to follow his or her own heart in these matters."

Every family has its weak spots, no matter how spiritual it may seem in other areas. In our own families, we must discover these spots and turn them back to the strength of God, in Jesus' name.

Genealogies often become controlling factors in the way people live and train their children. However, Christian couples should not rear their children this way. Believers need to break away from these ungodly hindrances and limitations, training their children in the victory and likeness of Christ! *Training* your children is your responsibility and your commitment to them. It means living in front of them, teaching them, and directing their lives by word and example. Training is not a smothering, overprotective, fearful control.

Now, lo, if he beget a son, that seeth all his father's sins which he hath done, and considereth, and doeth not such like,...he shall not die for the iniquity of his father, he shall surely live. (Ezekiel 18:14, 17)

A TIME FOR PARENTS TO LET GO

The book of Ecclesiastes says that there is a time for everything under the sun. (See Ecclesiastes 3:1.) That means that when children grow up and choose a life partner, it is time for parents to let go of them and to respect their marriage!

When parents refuse to do this, they cause major problems. When parents visit the newlyweds and tell them what they should or should not do, they cause problems. When grandchildren are born and the grandparents start telling the parents how to rear their children, they cause even more problems.

When a couple asks their parents or in-laws for advice, the parents should give it, but unless their advice is sought, parents should keep quiet and pray! Unfortunately, some parents can't wait to be consulted; they just barge in and tell their children how to live.

Parental interference causes friction in marriages, and that is how some marital problems begin. The tragedy is, some marriages never survive this interference because one of the partners is unable to break a parent's control over his or her life. I'm sad to say that some divorces are actually caused by interfering parents!

I am not saying that every in-law is a potential problem maker, but in-laws who attempt to control their children do cause problems. The most prevalent in-law problem is found in controlling parents who won't release their daughter or son. Such people have no trust in their own training of their children.

It is true that such parents are truly concerned about the proper training and upbringing of their offspring; the problem is that their sense of security and self-worth is vested in their son or daughter rather than in their own relationship with the living God. When the child is out on his own, it causes the parents to realize that their source of security, which is the child, is now lost—and they don't know what to do. They are no longer around him or her all the time to monitor and control his or her actions. They are living in such insecurity that they go into a frenzy!

Parents, if your children are married, release them to God. Look at the situation realistically. When you and your mate were first married, you had to find out how to live and make it together as one family. You both made right choices and wrong choices. You had rocky roads and smooth roads. You spent money wisely and sometimes foolishly. When the romance seemed to leave the marriage, you were stuck together by commitment until the romance sparked again. You had to discover together how to build a strong unit and call it a family.

Give your children the freedom to discover life with their mates on their own. If they come to you and your mate for advice, give it. But after it is given, leave your children alone to make their own decisions with their mates. Let them be responsible to live their own lives as adults. If you have trained your children by the Word of God, then you are not their foundation—God is, and you should rest in that fact.

Look at this time in your life as a fresh, new start of enjoyment for you and your mate. It is never too late to develop security in God and to begin a new adventure in life. It will take work, because so much of your married life has revolved around and centered upon your children; but you can do it. Allow the Holy Spirit to show you how to pray for your children's marriages and be a support to them. The days ahead can be the best ones of your life if you will make the right decision today to love, let go, and live.

CHAPTER

10

TEN

CONTROL BY SPOUSES

An overbearing husband destroys the life of his wife and children. An overbearing wife destroys the life of her husband and children. That's why many children leave home as soon as they reach the age of eighteen—or even younger! If parents do not leave room for their children to experience joy outside of their parental authority—if youngsters cannot live without their parents breathing down their necks all the time—the family will have problems.

No, I don't mean that children should be allowed to do whatever they want to do! This message must be understood in the Spirit in order to achieve a proper balance in life. People who don't have balance in their lives slide into errors of carnality or super-spirituality.

"SUBMIT, SUBMIT, SUBMIT!"

Some husbands who have no spiritual balance in their lives turn their wives into weary, battered nobodies. It is not exciting to live with a doormat. Most of these women were not that way when their husbands first met them. But eventually, because their mates were always yelling at them, "Submit,

submit, submit," they did. The constant demands and the abusive control they endured for so long finally caused them to submit to the point that now they barely exist. This is definitely *not* the plan of God for marriage. There are all sorts of insecurities that would cause a husband to dominate his wife in this way.

Some of these hurt and wounded wives decided that they needed to protect themselves, so they became involved in the feminist movement. Some joined because of ignorant, insensitive husbands who were always yelling at them, "Submit, submit, submit!"

On the other hand, some women are just as selfish and self-centered as these men. I once met a pastor's wife who did nothing but consume soft drinks and watch soap operas. She would not cook breakfast for her children, help them get off to school, or make any effort to clean the house. She didn't believe that any of these tasks were her job.

> **When there is love in marriage, there is mutual consideration and help.**

If a husband and wife will just flow together in the Spirit, there will be no question of "Whose job is this?" and "Whose job is that?" When there is love in a marriage, there is mutual consideration. The partners aren't selfish; they help each other.

There is a true, biblical attitude of submission on the part of a wife toward her husband. That kind of submission is of God, but it is nothing like what is demanded by a selfish, overbearing companion. I have met many women who cannot do anything unless their husbands approve of it. They live in constant fear of making their mates angry. Such women fear breathing without permission. They exist in a tight circle limited by the things their husbands allow them to do. All these women can say is, "Whatever you want, dear."

That's not being submissive; that's being a robot! Abusive control and domination cause the loss of human dignity. In such a marriage, the controlled partner doesn't become a "help mate"; he or she becomes a "slave mate." And that must stop.

This kind of dependent relationship is smothering and unnatural. It is based on insecurity and is in danger of destruction. Too much dependency will drive a person away. No one can protect his or her position and security by being overly dependent. God made us human beings to express life and to fulfill the purpose of our Creator in the earth. Anything that hinders that kind of life flow will eventually self-destruct.

Remember: God is our Source and Comfort in every area of life. Every prospering relationship stems from that revelation inside of us.

PORTRAIT OF A CONTROL VICTIM

Several years ago, as I was ministering in a church where I had been invited to speak, I met a woman who was, unfortunately, a perfect example of a control victim.

Before the service that evening, I was sitting at my book table in the back of the church because I like to talk with people. As I sat there, I watched this woman enter the building. She was pushing ahead of her, like a flock of geese, three rowdy children under five years of age. They were just toddlers, with all the energy and abandon of their age. They were doing everything all at the same time: screaming, hollering, laughing, and crying—the whole works. It takes two parents even to attempt to corral this many young dynamos, and this woman was trying to do it all alone.

Then I saw the door shut behind a man who had a mean look on his face. What I saw shocked my spirit. I thought to myself, *Something is wrong with this man. Maybe he's oppressed.*

The woman really had her hands full, so I walked down the aisle and helped her take off the children's coats. She didn't know that I was the visiting preacher. "I wonder where my husband is," she said with a strained look on her face. "Oh, there he is!"

Guess who the husband was: the man who had walked through the door and caused my spirit to sound off like an alarm, "There's something wrong...something wrong...something wrong...!" The man had already found a seat. He didn't even stand up to help his family enter the row. He pulled back his knees so they could squeeze through on their way to their seats. In the process, one youngster escaped and began running down the aisles. I picked him up and plopped him in his father's lap, saying, "Here's your child."

As I did so, I noticed that neither the wife nor the children were dressed very well, but the man was wearing a nice suit.

CONTROLLERS LIKE TO BE SERVED

Controllers try to act like God. Controlling spirits make people serve their own selfish needs and desires. Controllers never consider others. This is the hardest thing to get a controller to understand because, in his eyes, he is so wonderful and so right. He thinks he loves everybody because everybody serves him. This idea is totally false, of course.

That night I preached a sermon on control, and, to be perfectly honest, I directed it right at this man. After the time of worship, the woman came up to the front of the church and stood in the prayer line. As I laid hands on her and began to pray for her, I felt a reaction in her husband, even though he was still back in the congregation, and withdrew my hands from her.

We've got a big one here tonight! I thought. *This is a major controlling spirit.*

So I laid my hands on the woman's head again, and this time I was determined not to budge because I knew she wanted to be free. "I need your help," she whispered to me. "You're the first preacher who has let me know what I'm in. I thought my husband and I were living the way we were supposed to, but then I saw that other people's marriages were not like ours." This woman wasn't talking about material things. She was referring to the normal interaction between husband and wife: loving each other, holding hands, taking care of the children together—enjoying life with one another. That's what people get married for!

As I prayed for her, she got in the Spirit and began to be set free. Her face started to glow. But then something struck her soul with a shock! It was her husband's controlling spirit reacting.

"Don't get upset," I told her. "Just flow with the Spirit. God says that He wants you to be free."

It was almost half an hour before she was able to keep her freedom in the Spirit. By the anointing of God through prayer, she was able to see her value as a person. With the Word of God and scriptural counseling from their church, this couple's marriage was eventually made whole.

LEADERS SHOULD DEAL WITH CONTROLLERS

The leaders in that church should have dealt with that problem years earlier. We are brothers and sisters in Christ, and when there is a situation among us as bad as this one that goes on and on, the church elders and deacons should help the pastor confront it and restore liberty and peace to those affected by it. That is part of their job.

If you are forced to deal with a situation like this one, don't advertise the fact—just do it! The controlling husband or wife may react violently at first (any evil spirit will "blow up" when confronted directly), but deal with the problem with love and firmness in the power of the Holy Spirit.

CHAPTER
ELEVEN

CONTROL BY MONEY

J ust as control works most often through the *people* closest to the victim, so it also works through the *thing* closest to the one being controlled. The saying is true: "If God has your heart, He has your money." We must be sure that we direct our money; we must not allow money to direct us or dictate to us.

There is another saying: "He who pays the piper calls the tune." There is a great deal of truth to this quote as well. A number of people will be able to control you through money during your lifetime. It started when you were a child. Your parents exerted a certain amount of control over your behavior through your allowance. You were probably expected to perform certain tasks around the house in exchange for your allowance. Later in life, your bosses exerted a great deal of control over your behavior and job performance through your salary. These kinds of control through money are normal, as long as they are not excessive in any way.

Parents—especially well-to-do parents—also use money as a means to control their adult children. Spouses also use money as a lever of control—especially when both partners in a marriage work.

Another controlling influence that may never have occurred to you is debt. Being in debt means that you are, to some extent, under the control of other people. Debt can restrict the joy and achievement level of people's lives—and the pressure of debt can wreck marriages!

We must be cautious in the area of debt, that it does not consume us. Debt is a sneaky hindrance. It can creep upon us and ruin our lives if we are not wise to it. Satan can use this means to bind the church and hinder us from support-ing and giving to the work of the Lord around the world. We must be on our guard against this evil, because we are to finance the gospel in the earth. In this hour of shaky economy, we must oper-ate totally by God's laws of giving and receiving. (See Luke 6:38; Malachi 3:10.)

> **We must operate totally by God's laws of giving and receiving.**

Be wise in your financial and business dealings so you and your family can enjoy life on God's beau-tiful earth without the restraints of overwhelming debt.

CONTROL BY MONEY IN THE CHURCH

The above examples of financial control are common and often discussed. However, we will consider control through money in a far different way as it affects the local church.

Unfortunately, many churches frequently feature promi-nent members who are really caught up into controlling others with their money. They somehow think that if they give large tithes and offerings, then they have a right to issue orders. If everyone doesn't do exactly as they desire, they react.

If the pastor so much as preaches two minutes beyond twelve noon, they may threaten to reduce or withhold their offerings. If the pastor is not strong, and his security is in money, he may quickly buckle under to this type of financial pressure. He may agree to do anything demanded of him, without praying first or discussing the situation with the Lord, just to keep that large donation coming in! Such a pastor is depending upon flesh rather than on God.

Money is not head of the church—*Jesus Christ is!*

These prominent people need to learn that money is not given to the church to purchase power and prestige: Money is given to God as an expression of *love!*

The believer should establish tithing as a way of life. Giving is one means of showing God that we understand that He owns everything and that He has given good things to us and our household. We worship God with our money because of what it represents—total submission of our lives to Him. When we give our money, that act shows God, heaven, and the devil just who our Source is. Giving is a means of fulfilling a part of the covenant between us and the Lord, demonstrating that it is He who has given us the power to get wealth. (See Deuteronomy 8:18.)

Money is not head of the church— Jesus Christ is!

Now you may be thinking, *God didn't give me my money; I worked hard for it myself.* God gave you the breath of life so you could get up and go to work. He gave you strength to move and a brain to think creatively. If it were not for Him, you couldn't even go to work!

There is a whole world of revelation in the giving of money to God. Begin to ask the Holy Spirit to teach you the lifestyle of giving to God. Find the giving and tithing Scriptures in the Word of God, in both the Old and New Testaments. Study them and meditate on them until they become a revelation and a way of life to you.

God is not in a box, nor is He a taskmaster when it comes to giving. One particular couple had gotten into such terrible debt that they were unable to tithe and still continue living on a daily basis. They couldn't let even one bill go unpaid without destroying their future. So what did the Holy Spirit direct them to do? *Begin tithing toward the tithe!* This couple wanted so desperately to restore themselves in the area of giving that they began to tithe a small percentage toward what their normal tithe would be. They sowed seeds toward their financial restoration! As a result, today they give to their church over and above the required amount.

Be free in your giving so you can be free in your mind.

Money and debt do not have to control you. There is always a way, through the Holy Spirit, to recover. When I started preaching this message, money controllers began to react immediately! Do not let such people bother or hinder you. Do not allow money to control you. Be free in your giving so you can be free in your mind. When you see how God blesses your finances, you will grow in faith.

CONTROL HINDERS THE FLOW OF THE SPIRIT

One principle in which God carefully trained me in the beginning of my ministry is not to depend on people's giving to pay my ministry expenses. A frequent problem in the modern church is that some preachers depend upon people's giving. They get so controlled by money that they lose the real flow of the Spirit! This is one reason why some congregations are not going on with God. A few people with controlling spirits are running things in the church, and the pastor doesn't want to lose them because they are so influential in the city. However, their control, if not changed, will stop the move of God in that church!

Pastors have a need to be liked. Every person and every minister has that desire, but especially pastors because they are planted among the people they serve. Unlike the traveling evangelist, they can't come through town, blast out a sermon, and leave the next day! If a pastor is not secure in God, he will preach messages that the Lord has not told him to deliver, simply because he doesn't want to offend the influential, well-to-do members of his congregation. God doesn't instruct ministers to preach people-pleasing sermons.

As ministers, we must preach the fresh Word of the Lord; and it isn't always what the people want to hear! Having a big church is one thing, but compromising to have one produces a large, stagnant church without the power and glory of God.

A minister must realize that God is his Source, not a prominent person with money. If you are a minister who is being controlled by someone with money in your church, this is what you should do: Hand the money back and say to those who are attempting to control you with it, "Here's your money. God is my Source. If your motive in giving is not to use your money to serve the Lord and His church, then go someplace else where you can do what you want."

And that is what that person will do—he won't come to church for a while. He may not even speak to you, but if he does, he will say things like, "Who do you think you are, coming to our town? I was here long before you were ever voted in, Pastor!"

Here's something important to remember: *Pastors are not voted in; God sets them in the church.* Furthermore, the pastor—not the flock—is the undershepherd of that congregation. The elders and deacons are to give the pastor counsel, advice, and physical and spiritual support, but the pastor is not obligated to follow that counsel and advice if the Spirit of God leads otherwise.

USING MONEY TO CONTROL THE PREACHER

I had an interesting experience with one of these controlling types once. He offered me money if I would get up and retract what I had just preached about removing proud members of the church board! I had said, "If a deacon or an elder cannot flow with the Spirit of God, then he should be removed from the board."

After this man had offered me the bribe, I replied, "I won't retract what I said because it was right. But you can give me the money anyway." He didn't do it. I found out later that he was the problem in the church! This man wanted me to retract that statement and the anointed words that convicted people of their sin. He wanted to see if he could manipulate me.

Sometimes people come up to me after a service, complaining to me and wanting me to withdraw something I have said. If I am wrong about something, I will apologize. If I have said something that is not right, I will retract the statement. However, I will not withdraw from the anointing, and I will not apologize for being right.

If you apologize for something you said while under the anointing, it weakens your anointing and power. It causes you to falter in your stand and strength. The truth is the truth. When you stand with the truth, you will be right with God and right with the people.

CHAPTER TWELVE

HOW TO BE FREE FROM CONTROL

There is freedom for those who are bound by control. Whether you have been the controller or the person being controlled, you can be set free! Regardless of the degree of control you are under, you need to be set free, because you can't live a happy, normal life if you are being controlled by someone else.

How do you break the power of control? You must break your habit of unnatural expectations toward another person. You must break the power of fear over you, in Jesus' name.

STEPS TOWARD FREEDOM

If you are being controlled by someone else, here are some steps you can take to free yourself from that situation.

1. Recognize that you are being controlled.

Let's examine some of the ways you can know if you are being controlled by another person.

First, when you are around the other individual, you are not yourself. You feel intimidated, and you grow increasingly ill at ease around him or her. You wish your relationship were as happy and free as others you see.

Second, you feel insecure and inadequate when you try to do new things on your own. Your hopes can be totally dashed and your mind thrown into confusion and instability if the other person makes just one negative statement, such as, "I don't think you can do that."

Third, you feel obligated to spend time with the other person, even though he or she has no consideration for your schedule or lifestyle. As soon as you return from a pleasant outing with friends or acquaintances, the other person, because he or she was not invited, feels threatened and attacks you. The individual may even try to "spiritualize" the attack by saying, "I've been in the Spirit, and I know what went on while you were gone." He or she will offer you a list of things about you that aren't true. If you aren't careful, you will end up agreeing with him or her.

Finally, when you are pulled between two opinions, yours and the other person's, you feel obligated to agree. You lose your human dignity to the point that you become careless about your appearance and lose your desire to be successful in life. You look and feel listless and exhausted.

2. Recognize how that person controls you.

Is it through fear, guilt, obligation, anger, tears, frustration, confusion, or any of the other things we have discussed? Whatever it may be, find it and break its power over you, in Jesus' name. Locate the Scriptures that strengthen you against these negative influences. Say them aloud over and over until they become a part of you. When the controlling attack comes, you will then be able to counterattack it through the Word of God.

3. **Determine and apply the correction you need in your thought patterns and actions in order to stop the control from dominating your life.**

For example, if you are controlled through silence, learn not to respond to it. Don't feel guilty when the controller doesn't speak to you for days on end. Go on and enjoy life. Let the other person be miserable if that is what he or she chooses. Sooner or later the controller will realize that silence can no longer be an effective method to control you.

Often a husband will refuse to speak to his wife (or vice versa) because of something she said that he didn't agree with. He uses this childish weapon to punish her instead of discussing the problem like an adult and resolving the issue so they can live in peace and harmony. It is against God's perfect will for two people to live together in the same house with this kind of strife going on between them. (See Proverbs 20:3.)

The Holy Spirit will not flow through a clogged pipe!

Disharmony hinders the movement of the Spirit of God. Even if a tiny "irk" occurs among my ministerial staff, we deal with it and get rid of it immediately because we know that *the Holy Spirit will not flow through a clogged pipe!* When you are grieved and hurt, the Holy Spirit cannot speak or heal through you. In order to hear accurately in the Spirit realm, you must be free from the hurts and bondage that may come in life.

Another way a controller may try to dominate you is through words of inadequacy or failure, such as, "You can't do that; you don't know how. You'll just fail because you're not educated." Remind the controller that Abraham Lincoln suffered nothing but defeats and setbacks for years before he became a successful statesman and many people thought that Albert Einstein was mentally retarded as a child. In fact, many of the most successful people in life never earned an academic degree. So don't let your past history of failures or your lack of formal education keep you from becoming all that God intends for you.

A controller may even use threats against you, such as, "If you don't do what I say, I'm going to leave you!" Don't be intimidated by such negative remarks. Remember that the Greater One lives in you and that you are important to God. Attack those evil spirits by reminding them of who you are in Christ Jesus. Again, find Scriptures to support you in your battle. Matthew 4:10 is a good one. The devil came to Jesus demanding that He fall down and worship him. Jesus answered, *"Get thee hence, Satan: for it is written, Thou shalt worship the Lord thy God, and him only shalt thou serve."* Do as Jesus did and quote the Word of God to your adversary Satan.

Control equals idolatry. When a person who is controlled is secure only in the relationship with his or her controller, it amounts to a form of idolatry. Because both individuals in that relationship look to each other as their security, they become one another's god. That is idolatry! Matthew 4:10, which I have just mentioned, is just one Scripture that will sever this kind of control.

If you are under the abusive control of another individual, you need to deal with that situation. Both you and your controller are miserable anyway. Why not get things right with

God? To do this, you will have to learn to pray and break the power of the controlling spirit—and all the spirits that go with it, such as fear, guilt, obligation, confusion, and frustration.

When you break the grip of control over your life, it doesn't mean that you won't experience a certain degree of loneliness. Those controlling spirits will storm out of your life, and you will be left sitting all alone. The first thing that will strike you is a feeling of guilt, followed by fear that you are not capable of making it on your own. You will begin to ask yourself, "What am I going to do now?"

Keep using your authority to rebuke guilt and fear in the name of Jesus.

Don't panic. And don't give up. Stop in your tracks and say, "Devil, move, in Jesus' name! I break your power over me. Get off of me. You are a liar!" Keep using your authority to rebuke guilt and fear in the name of Jesus. (See 2 Timothy 1:7.) Realize that control is not just a natural psychological problem; it is also a spiritual problem. As we noted earlier, human nature is naturally controlling. But when control becomes unnatural, it is demonic, and you must fight it every day.

It doesn't matter whether you feel that you are no longer under guilt or fear, you still must be on your guard. When you get up in the morning, make sure that the first thing you do is to tell those controlling spirits to leave you alone. Break their power over you. Command them to go from you, in Jesus' name. Quote Scriptures to them and make them obey you. The next time you meet the controller, he or she may not speak to you because you haven't been in contact or asked for help. But don't dare feel guilty or try to make up. You have just won your freedom, so enjoy it!

4. Confront your controller.

First comes the initial break from the controlling person. After you are strong in the Spirit, and you know that your heart is right, then you can take the final step in your complete deliverance from control: confronting your controller!

THE BATTLE OF CONFRONTATION

Confrontation does not always have to be a battle. But you must be strong when confronting a controller because controllers are not the most logical people to deal with. They have been blinded by their own insecurities. You must say to your controller, "You have controlled me in these ways (name them). I love you, but these things will not work in my life anymore. You must change or we can no longer have a relationship."

When you do this, several things are likely to happen. As soon as you accuse the other person of controlling you, he or she will probably protest, "I'm not trying to control you. I love you. Everything I have done has been for your benefit. Do you mean to tell me that you don't appreciate it?" Or the controller will turn the tables on you and try to hide his or her mistakes and wrongs by making it appear that everything that has happened has been your fault.

If you are not strong, you will slip from your stand in the Spirit into the soulish realm, which is an emotional realm. The controller will continue, "You know I love you; we just have to work this out." You will burst into tears and say, "Oh, I know." Then you will be back in the clutches of control again!

The controller will manifest all sorts of strong emotions: anger, jealousy, pride, fear, and many others. No normal human being could change emotions so quickly; this is further evidence of the controlling spirits at work within that individual. If you are really strong in the Lord, you can watch and call the name of each spirit as it is manifested.

Know this: You are in a war, not on a vacation. If you are weak, you had better call in a team of strong prayer warriors to back you in intercession as you enter this battle.

After the confrontation is over, don't sit and meditate about what has happened. Don't think about it at all! Shut it out of your mind. Instead of dwelling on it and rehashing it over and over again, get up and walk around the room, praying as you go.

THE PRICE

Some are not willing to pay the price to go on with the Lord. They would rather stay in their own little ruts and not have to be concerned with change. If you truly desire to go on with God, then you may well have to pay this price. You may have to make the very difficult decision to turn loose of friends or other close associates who do not choose to go on and who will oppose your doing so.

You will continue to love them, pray for them, communicate with them, and even visit them. However, with love and firmness, you will not allow them to hinder you or dissuade you from doing what you have to do to fulfill your godly call and purpose.

Do not bow to or serve the insecurities in another person. Do not allow fear to abort your destiny, your mission for God in the earth. Be bold and be strong: Walk in the compassion of God and take the nations in His name.

LEARNING TO SAY NO WITHOUT FEELING GUILTY

CONTENTS

LEARNING TO SAY NO WITHOUT FEELING GUILTY

1. Saying No 105

2. The First No.. 108

3. Say No to the Flesh...................................... 110

4. No Is Not Maybe 112

5. No Cannot Always Be Nice 115

6. Power, Not Politics 118

7. Grounds for True Fellowship.................... 121

8. Say No to a Wandering Mind 123

9. Say No to Your Children 125

10. No in the New Testament 129

11. No Must Be Said in Love............................ 132

12. No Means Taking a Stand 134

13. When to Say No... 137

14. Reasons Why People Do Not Say No 141

15. Five No Facts 148

16. No Affects Destinies 150

CHAPTER

1

ONE

SAYING NO

The world has discovered the value of the word *no*. The secular media has made *no* a household word by popularizing the "Just Say No" drug campaign. They advertised the slogan on television, radio, and billboards, and in magazines and newspapers. Finally, the world has realized the importance of saying no to some things.

However, it is time the church of Jesus Christ rediscovered this very important, priceless word—this little but very powerful word. After all, God was the first to advocate the concept for which the word stands: denying Satan, denying the bondage others seek to hold you in, and denying self. Every preacher and every lay person needs to learn to say no. In fact, every human being needs to learn to say no.

Undoubtedly everyone has been in a situation where he wished he had said no instead of yes. However, because he had given his word, he went ahead and did whatever was involved. He kept his "contract." Perhaps saying yes not only led to inconvenience but to sin. He did not sin by breaking his word, but perhaps he sinned by grumbling and complaining or by criticizing and finding fault. Perhaps he sinned by getting into resentment and bitterness, or even in unforgiveness toward the other person or people involved.

Many people seem to be afraid to say no. They seem to equate the word *no* with negative things and with a lack of fun or joy in life. Nothing could be further from the truth.

CHECK YOUR JOY AND PEACE GAUGES

The Bible says, *"Restore unto me the joy of thy salvation"* (Psalm 51:12).

Christians should have joy, vitality, and fun in what they are doing. If there is no joy, something is very wrong. There is joy in God's presence, and if you are doing what is right (His will), you are in His presence, and He is in your presence.

> **Christians should have joy, vitality, and fun in what they are doing.**

Every now and then we need to check up on our joy and peace gauges as we drive down the road called Life. If those gauges are on empty, we need to get refilled. We should not let our joy and peace run low any more than we would the gasoline in our vehicles.

Phyllis Mackall of Tulsa, Oklahoma, is not only a member of my board of directors but a precious friend. The daughter of a Pentecostal minister, she is very knowledgeable about Pentecostal history. In addition, she has wisdom. When she talks, I listen.

Once, she told me, "There are two things every person in the ministry needs to learn to say: no and thank you."

Her advice was both wise and true. If we say yes when it should have been no, we get into trouble; and when we forget to show appreciation to people, we cause trouble and hurt.

Everyone needs to say no and thank you more often. How often have we said no and gotten into trouble? Usually, more trouble comes from saying yes. We need to learn to say no without feeling guilty about it. Sometimes *no* is God's anointed answer for a situation.

If we begin saying no, soon we will know how to say it and smile. No is a wonderful word. Phyllis helped me learn the value of that little, powerful word. I would go over to her house, and she would say, "Roberts, what's the anointed word?"

I would say, "No."

And she would say, "That's not loud enough. That's not strong enough. You don't believe it quite yet. Say it again."

She would have me say it over and over until it came out loud, strong, and bold.

"That's it. You've got it," she would finally say.

Sometimes you have to yell something to make every part of you hear it. If you speak softly, what you say seems to carry no weight, even with yourself. Learn to say no boldly.

Let's look at the first example in the Bible of people who said yes when they should have said no and suffered serious consequences. God has never been afraid of the word *no*. The Bible uses that word over and over again from Genesis to Revelation.

CHAPTER

TWO

THE FIRST NO

G od told Adam and Eve, "You can eat from any tree except one."

"No," God said, "you may not eat of this one tree."

We all know what happened when they disobeyed God's no. Was God being mean? Certainly not. His prohibition came for their own protection. No is often a word of protection for our personal lives, our families, our businesses, our churches, and our nations. God has His children's best interests in mind when He says no.

The serpent came along and tried to turn God's no into a yes. He told Eve the fruit was good for her because it would make her just like God. Instead of yelling "No!" at the devil, Eve began to think, "Well, that fruit does look good. God could not have really meant for us not to eat it."

Yes, He did. When God says no, He means no. When He says yes, He means yes. But Eve ate the fruit and gave some to Adam, who then had his chance to say no and turn things around. But Adam put Eve before God and joined her in eating the fruit. The consequence was that both lost everything. If Adam and Eve had obeyed God's first no, they would still be in the garden of Eden, eating, having fun, and enjoying life. They could have continued to live in perfect joy, but they lost everything.

When you allow your mind to be enticed by what is not the will of God, you will soon act on that enticement. What you think about, you will soon do. Adam ate the fruit and was miserable (the state of all those who say yes when they should have said no). Success

When God says no, He means no. When He says yes, He means yes.

is not built on how many times you say yes. Usually, success is built on how many times you say a strong no—and stick to it. A weak no too easily can be turned into a yes.

NO RUNS FROM THE APPEARANCE OF EVIL

No has legs. It is a force that runs from the appearance of evil. Those who say no do not walk with the ungodly, stand with sinners, nor sit with those who are scornful of God's ways. (See Psalm 1:1.) No never stays in a place where evil abounds.

No has actions and a big voice. The Bible says if we do not do what we know to do, we have sinned. (See James 4:17.) Not saying no when we know to do so is sin.

No stops conflicts of doubt and guilt. No has no suspicion in it. Often, no is very hard to say, but once you have said it, you will feel like a giant. You will be happy and proud of yourself.

CHAPTER

3

THREE

SAY NO TO THE FLESH

L et's look at another biblical example: Samson. (See Judges 14.)

God used Samson mightily. When the anointing came on him, he had strength no one else had. He could easily get the best of the Philistines. He was so strong that he could do nearly anything he wanted to do. He was respected by everyone, greatly esteemed by the leaders of Israel, and feared by the leaders of the Philistines.

He had a big problem, however. He would not say no to his flesh. He liked beautiful women, and the sad thing is that he preferred pagan women. Probably, he could have had any marriageable girl he wanted from among the Israelites, but he only wanted foreign women.

He said to his father, "Go over there to that other nation and get that woman for me."

His parents asked, "What is wrong with you? Why can't you find a girl among our own people whom you would like to have as your wife?"

Then Samson threw a tantrum. Flesh always has tantrums, just as children do.

If you are a parent who knows how to say no and keep your word, you can look at a child having a tantrum and say, "Now that is enough! Stop that right now," and your child will stop.

But Samson's father did not do that. He gave in to his son's demands.

First of all, Samson should have said no to himself. Before you can say no to anyone else, you have to learn to say it to yourself. Before you can look someone else straight in the eye, say no, and **Before you can say no to anyone else, you have to learn to say it to yourself.** not feel guilty about it, you must learn to deny your own mind and your own flesh. Then it becomes a lot easier to say no to others.

Also, you need to remember this: Silence usually means yes in people's minds. You need to verbalize your stand.

Learn to make your body walk the bedroom floor and pray, even when it rises up and screams, "I want to sleep."

Say, "No, I am going to pray in tongues for an hour and enjoy every minute of it." Then do it.

CHAPTER

4

FOUR

NO IS NOT MAYBE

*N*o is a spiritual word, and spiritual words are absolutes. There is no maybe and no wondering in the realm of the Spirit. Most people do not like that, however. If you stand on your yeas and your nays (see Matthew 5:37), they will say you are into spiritual pride. The world basically is very wishy-washy, but the church should not be following the same path. We need to say no a lot stronger than we have been saying it.

There is no neutrality in the spiritual world, no summit meetings in order to find a compromise. Heaven and hell are white and black. There is no gray, no lukewarmness. Jesus said to be hot or cold, or He would spew you out of His mouth. (See Revelation 3:15–16.) His words are absolutes, and our words need to become absolute again. Words are important.

Later, after his marriage to one pagan woman ended in her betraying him, Samson listened to his desire for the forbidden. Saying yes to Delilah did not stop with the sin of cohabitating with a pagan woman. It led to dire consequences for Samson and for Israel. (See Judges 16.)

She began to ask Samson, "Where does your strength come from?"

Instead of saying, "No. I am not going to tell you, so don't ever ask me again," Samson tried to put her off with jokes and then lies. But she would not be put off.

"If you love me, you'll tell me. You are making a fool out of me," she said.

The Bible relates that she kept pressing him daily so that his soul was vexed. In other words, she kept nagging him until he did not know what was right and what was wrong. Finally he gave in and told her what she wanted to know, although he knew it was a bad idea.

God's words are absolutes, and our words must become absolutes again.

Samson would not say no to himself or to Delilah. He woke up one morning with his eyes poked out and spent the rest of his life like a donkey grinding meal. Even though his death was a final triumph, his life was shortened and his work for the Lord, defeated.

"DELILAH" IS AROUND TODAY

Some people want explanations for your no so they can find a way to trick you by your own words. They are "Delilahs" who search for a crack in your words in order to cause your no to become a yes. People like that are sly as snakes. They slither in and poke their heads in places they have no business being. Then you are surprised they got there.

When you say no, the windows will crash down, the blinds will be drawn, and the doors will slam shut and lock. If you are strong in your answer and do not waver, no one can slither in and change your mind. They might pound and knock, but they cannot get in because *no* has been declared. When it is spoken with spiritual force, it cannot be penetrated.

In this hour, we are going through the greatest war the church has ever had in the natural and in the spiritual realms. A lot of the battles would not even occur if we would just make a bold proclamation to the evil spirits: "No, you cannot come in here. No, you cannot do that." No...period. That would stop unnecessary battles. Say no more often, and you will not have to pray a half-million words trying to get victory. Say no, decree it, and stand on it.

No is a wonderful word. It is too bad Samson did not know how wonderful it is. He did not fulfill his destiny because he would not say no. If you do not say no to yourself, you will not say no to the "Delilahs."

CHAPTER

5

FIVE

NO CANNOT ALWAYS BE NICE

King Saul was another person who did not value this little two-letter word as he should have. God commanded Saul to attack the Amalekites and *"utterly destroy all that they have"* (1 Samuel 15:3).

> *Then came the word of the LORD unto Samuel, saying, It repenteth me that I have set up Saul to be king: for he is turned back from following me, and hath not performed my commandments. And it grieved Samuel; and he cried unto the LORD all night.* (verses 10–11)

Verses 13 through 21 tell us that Samuel came to Saul and asked, "Have you done what God commanded?"

Saul lied, "I have done all the Lord has commanded."

Then Samuel said, "What is the bleating of the sheep and the lowing of the oxen that I hear?"

He confronted Saul, "Stop, and let me tell you what the Lord told me tonight."

But when Saul was confronted, he blamed the people. Sounds like Adam again, doesn't it? Or perhaps it sounds like Aaron excusing himself for not telling the people no when they wanted a golden calf. (See Exodus 32:22–24.)

Saul told Samuel the people had made him keep back some of the choice animals from slaughter in order to sacrifice them to God. That was so ridiculous. Saul was the king, and people then had to obey the king.

There was power in the words of a king. He could have a man put to death if the man displeased him. All Saul had to do was say no to the people, but he feared their opinion of him, and he let his no become a yes. Saul probably thought, "Samuel's not being reasonable here. I will be nice to the people."

BEING NICE MAY COST YOU

Being nice cost Saul dearly, and it cost his people dearly. It cost him not only his throne, but his life and the lives of his sons!

You cannot live in a place of compromise or neutrality with God. You are either all the way in, or you are not in at all. Without God's absolutes, we will never walk in the realm of the Spirit. We must learn to say no to the desires of the flesh, to the world, to the devil, and to other people who would lead us away from God and His ways.

> **We must learn to say no to the desires of the flesh and all that will lead us away from God.**

We should learn from the examples in the Bible. The mistakes made by biblical leaders are written down for our example and can save us hours of heartache. The word *no* can especially save pastors hours of heartache. How many times has a pastor said yes to someone and allowed that person to preach from his pulpit knowing he should have said no? Then it takes him hours to undo what one man does in five minutes from the pulpit—all because the pastor did not want to hurt someone's feelings. For lack of a no, the sheep were exposed to error, division, or false spirits.

I have been in some churches where people have said to the pastor, "We want to come to your church." The pastor had agreed, although he knew those people would not be good members, and they destroyed the church. He did not want to hurt their feelings, but a church split hurt worse and hurt more people than saying no in the beginning would have.

Basically, all of us want to be nice, and we want everyone to like us. We must love everyone, but we do not have to accept all that comes with everyone. God loves the world but hates sin. He accepts the sinner but rejects the sin.

CHAPTER
6
SIX

POWER, NOT POLITICS

Christians must make a decision: Are they going to be political or powerful?

God is powerful, but He is not political. Politics is false power. Religious politics is one of the major traps ministries need to avoid. Religious politics gives people a false sense of power and influence. If you "play politics," you may think you have influence, but it will not last. The person who put you in position can pull the rug out from under you and stop you from giving out the Word of the Lord. Do not be political. Just be powerful in the Lord.

Politicians rarely, if ever, use no or yes. Instead, they say, "Let's discuss it." In religious politics, as well, there is never a right or a wrong. There is only whoever is the strongest or whoever has the most power and money. People who go the route of religious politics do and say things simply to please others, usually to gain something. That is why they do not like Christians who move in the prophetic flow of the Lord.

Prophets or those who operate prophetically stand on the Word of God and say, "This is truth. This is the absolute standard. What you are saying or doing is wrong."

Those rebuked many times will reply, "How do you know? You are in pride."

Truth is truth. When you agree with it, you are right. When you disagree, you are wrong. When I preach the Word of God, I am right. If I preach personal convictions, I could be wrong. When I preach chapter and verse, it is right, and I do not have to apologize for it. I do not have to withdraw and consider what people are going to think of me. As long as I preach the truth, God will give me success. It is the same for anyone else. Preach the truth, and do not waver.

GOD DOES NOT ACCEPT MAYBE

God has a yes and a no. When you stand before Him, you are either saved or you are not. You will not be able to get away with a maybe. You will not be able to figure how many good deeds equal a yes. Accepting Jesus is the only way to salvation. If you are not saved, it does not matter how many services you have been to or how many good deeds you have done.

> **God has a yes and a no. His truth is truth.**

Some people say, "You are too harsh. That scares people. That offends people." But I would rather tell people the truth and risk offending them than not tell the truth and be responsible for them going to hell. If it is not yes with heaven, they are going to hell.

Some people blush at the word *hell*. There is hell, and there is a heaven, and there is no in-between. There is no neutrality with God.

Political people do not like "yes or no" people. When people who take strong stands meet political people, there is usually a battle. Political people always want to have a summit meeting to discuss ideas, opinions, and so on. They say they want a neutral balance, when all they really want is for you to compromise and agree with them. You cannot balance the truth. Truth is already as balanced as it is ever going to be.

CHAPTER

7

SEVEN

GROUNDS FOR TRUE FELLOWSHIP

There is a strong movement today toward church unity. Part of that movement is of God, but part of it is not. What are the grounds for Christian fellowship? What is true Christian fellowship?

I see three ingredients that are necessary for true fellowship:

1. Those in agreement must respect one another.

2. They must believe the same things.

3. They must have the same desires for the kingdom.

If you do not respect someone else, you cannot really fellowship with him. Without equal respect for one another's integrity and spiritual strength, imbalance results. Also, you do not have true fellowship unless both parties believe the same things. Otherwise, it will be a false unity, and conflict will result sooner or later.

True Christian fellowship means you have the same desires for the kingdom. Some people do not concern themselves with furthering God's kingdom on earth at all. Some want to establish their own little kingdoms. They may say they minister for God's kingdom, but they really do not. Therefore, if you sincerely want to work for God, how can you unite with someone trying to build his kingdom at the expense of God's? You cannot. The "unity" would not work. It would be false.

There are those who say, "Yes, but we can fellowship together without agreeing on everything. We just will not talk about those things we do not agree on."

Have you ever tried that? Eventually the differences create a conflict. The Word says, *"Can two walk together, except they be agreed?"* (Amos 3:3). You can pretend to agree with someone, but if you really do not, your disagreements—talked about or not—will affect your fellowship. For true Christian unity, these three things must be present in a relationship.

> **For true Christian unity, mutual respect, desire, and belief must be present.**

Christians certainly cannot have fellowship with those who are not part of God's family. *"What fellowship has light with darkness?"* (2 Corinthians 6:14 NASB). Your light will grow dim the longer you fellowship with those in darkness. There is no way you can have real fellowship with people who are not walking in light.

CHAPTER 8

EIGHT

SAY NO TO A WANDERING MIND

David is a prime example of a man who did not say no and later was deeply grieved because he had not. Eve could be blamed in Adam's case, but the woman in this case could not be blamed. It was all David's fault.

First of all, as king, David should have been out leading his men in the battle, instead of staying at home.

> *And it came to pass, after the year was expired, at the time when kings go forth to battle, that David sent Joab, and his servants with him, and all Israel; and they destroyed the children of Ammon, and besieged Rabbah. But David tarried still at Jerusalem.*   (2 Samuel 11:1)

Second, David should not have had so much idle time on his hands. He was sitting around looking for something to do. Idle time almost always means devil's time. That does not mean you have to be going ninety miles an hour working yourself to death. But it does mean that you do not sit around and let your mind wander where it will. David was being lazy. His mind began to wander, and as he sat on the rooftop, he saw Bathsheba bathing. He should have yelled, "No, flesh! No."

Instead, he sent for her to come visit him. Because David was the king, she had to obey him. He misused his authority to gratify his own flesh. That was bad enough, but unfortunately, it did not stop there. To cover his first sin, he committed another—murder. He had Bathsheba's husband killed.

> **If you give in to the flesh in small ways, before you know it, you are in sin.**

That is the terrible thing about indulging the flesh. If you give in to it in small ways, before you know it, you are giving in to the flesh in greater ways.

ALL SINS LEAD TO BIGGER SINS

All David had to do was say no, and it would have been anointed. The small sin of saying yes to his eyes led to saying yes to his body and then yes to murder. Consequently, God sent his prophet Nathan to correct David. The result is that the child born of David and Bathsheba's sin died. Moreover, David's family was continually at war and Israel was divided. Sin does not pay.

David's sin has never been forgotten. Even the world remembers it, and of course, magnifies it. Today, most people can tell you that David was a murderer and adulterer, but they forget that he was a great king of Israel and a man after God's own heart! What a way to be remembered! The names of David and Bathsheba have been bywords for saying yes to the flesh for thousands of years. If they had simply said no, their names would be associated with godly things and not sin. God's people must learn to say no to the flesh.

CHAPTER

9

NINE

SAY NO TO YOUR CHILDREN

A nother area where people do not say no often enough is to their children. Many great men throughout history have lost their anointing, and sometimes their ministries, because they did not raise their children according to biblical principles. One of those is also found in the books of Samuel.

> *Now the sons of Eli were sons of Belial* [or sons of the devil]; *they knew not the LORD.* (1 Samuel 2:12)

Eli's sons knew not the Lord. Why not? Why didn't Eli teach and train them up in the Lord? Why did he let them do whatever they wanted? Because he never learned to say no to them. Look what happened:

> *Wherefore the sin of the young men* [Eli's sons] *was very great before the LORD: for men abhorred the offering of the LORD. But Samuel ministered before the LORD, being a child....Moreover his mother made him a little coat, and brought it to him from year to year, when she came up with*

her husband to offer the yearly sacrifice.

(1 Samuel 2:17-19)

Notice, we have two kinds of people in this situation. The sons of Eli were born into his lineage of the priesthood. They were expected to be pure and upright. But they were not. Then there was Samuel, who was not born into the priesthood but brought into it. If you read 1 Samuel 2, you will see that he lived a different kind of life before the Lord than Eli did. As he was dedicated to the Lord's service and grew up in the house of the Lord under Eli, he lived a holy, pure life.

After he grew older, Samuel told Eli that his sons were using their office of priest to entice the women of Israel into illicit sex. (See 1 Samuel 2:22.) They also were taking portions of the animals brought for offerings that by law were not allocated to the priesthood. (See 1 Samuel 2:13-17.)

SIN OF ELI'S SONS CONTINUES

The sons of the high priest, the prophet Eli, were having sex at the door of the tabernacle! This sin still goes on today. Adultery among the ministry and in the church is just as much an abomination to God as it was then. Sexual sins have caused more problems in Christians and in religious matters than most of us know.

What did Eli do? He said,

Nay, my sons; for it is no good report that I hear: ye make the Lord's people to transgress. (1 Samuel 2:24)

Well, "Whoop-de-doo!" He should have taken authority over the situation, whatever it took, and said a firm no to his sons. Instead of slapping them on their wrists and saying,

"Naughty, naughty," Eli should have removed them from serving until they repented and changed their ways. His no should have been so loud, bold, and strong that there was no question of the consequences if they continued in their sins. Eli learned the hard way that *no is anointed.*

A man of God came to Eli with a prophecy of judgment from the Lord: "I told you to take care of your sons. Because you did not take care of your sons, I am going to remove you and your lineage from this position." (See 1 Samuel 2:27–36.) Eli did not say no to his sons, so they lost their lives and he lost the priesthood for his

> **Eli learned the hard way that no is anointed.**

descendants. Eli's sons caused the Lord's people to transgress, and Eli never dealt with the problem. Because he did not, he was removed along with them.

What a sad ending for Eli! All because he did not put his foot down and say, "No, my sons, you will not do these things anymore."

HOPE DOES NOT REPLACE NO

We still have the same problem today with a lot of ministries and in a lot of Christian homes. People are not saying no to their children. They are not saying no to the things of the devil designed to split their families. People just hope everything will work out. Hoping will not solve the problem. Not saying no will destroy you! It will cause you to lose everything. The Bible shows examples of this over and over!

The truly amazing thing about the story of Eli and his sons is that Samuel, who grew up seeing the situation and was even used by God to warn Eli, allowed the same problem to develop in his own family! God used him mightily to warn another man about not saying no, then he turned around and committed the same sin.

Samuel did not say no to his own children, and they did evil in the sight of the Lord. Samuel followed in Eli's footsteps and did not do a thing to stop his sons. Of all people, Samuel knew how to use the anointed word *no*. Through watching David, Saul, and Eli, he saw firsthand the consequences of saying yes or a weak no. Yet he fell into the same trap.

No is a protection from heaven. If you will use it and let your communication be yes and no with no discussion, you will walk in victory. Right is right, and wrong is wrong. Your words will align you with whichever way you choose.

When you say no to your children, mean it. They may whine and mope, but *no* gives them security. Your child may want that fourth cookie, but tell him, "No, you can't have another cookie." Whine, whine, whine, and your cute little boy may reach for it again. Don't let him. Say no. He may not like it now, but when he grows up with standards and a sense of security, he will come home in later years and say, "Thanks, Mom and Dad."

When you go to his house, you will see his children being brought up right. You will see him saying no when he should. He learned it from you!

CHAPTER

TEN

NO IN THE NEW TESTAMENT

We have looked at several examples from the Old Testament where people did not use no properly. However, one of the best examples of someone who should have said no is found in the New Testament. That man was Judas. His flesh and his greed said yes, yes, yes, and he ended in destruction. In Luke 22:3–6, we read,

> *Then entered Satan into Judas surnamed Iscariot, being of the number of the twelve. And he went his way, and communed with the chief priests and captains, how he might betray him unto them. And they were glad, and covenanted to give him money. And he promised, and sought opportunity to betray him unto them in the absence of the multitude.*

Judas could have said no to the greed in his soul. He could have said no to the chief priests who besought him. When people begin seeking you with wrong motives, stop them with a loud, bold, strong NO.

This is especially true for young ministries. People with wrong motives murder a lot of ministries in their infancy. If a person wants to help you, but that person's heart is not right, you had better have the backbone to say no. If you do not, you will be very sorry. I learned this the hard way, and I have learned to say no.

NO CAN PROTECT YOU

No is a protection for you. It can protect the call of God on your life, your destiny, your family, and your church. *No* does not need an explanation. It just needs to be *no*.

Judas could have said, "No, I will not betray the King of Kings." But he did betray Him. Then Judas went out and hanged himself. Saying yes when he should have said no caused him so much guilt and shame that he took his own life. *No* would have prevented that from happening.

> **No can protect the call of God on your life, destiny, family, and church.**

Contrast Judas' life and death with Peter's. Peter also betrayed Jesus. In fact, Peter ran and hid when Jesus was taken away and then denied Him three times (Mark 14:66–72.) He had more concern for what people thought of him and for his own safety than for his relationship with Christ. He was so concerned that he refused to take a stand for Him.

He should have declared, "Yes, I know Him."

His yes was a no, and his no was a yes. Peter really was confused. However, he did repent. Judas could have repented, but he did not. Peter repented, and it was not too late for him. Peter turned his no into a no and his yes into a yes. He became a strong man for God and was used mightily in

130

the Lord's work. His life ended in a blaze of glory and not through suicide.

Another New Testament example where *no* was not used properly is in 2 Timothy 4:10: *"For Demas hath forsaken me, having loved this present world."*

Paul had been training this man, Demas. What a privilege for Demas. Can you imagine the honor of being personally trained by Paul? Demas apparently did not appreciate this honor, however, for he refused to say no to the desires of his flesh and to the pull of the world. To fulfill his own lust, he left the greatest revivalist that the world has ever known, this man Paul.

Think of what it must have been like to sit at Paul's feet and learn how to turn nations upside down. Demas was learning from the man who wrote half the New Testament. But he loved this present world more. His flesh screamed yes, and he went with that. First John 2:15–17 says,

Love not the world, neither the things that are in the world. If any man love the world, the love of the Father is not in him. For all that is in the world, the lust of the flesh, and the lust of the eyes, and the pride of life, is not of the Father, but is of the world. And the world passeth away, and the lust thereof: but he that doeth the will of God abideth for ever.

We have to say no to our desires, to the flesh, to this world, and to people, circumstances, and devils. *No* is anointed.

CHAPTER
11
ELEVEN

NO MUST BE SAID IN LOVE

Many times, we think people who say no are just being mean. However, saying no at the right time and place is not mean. Sometimes, saying yes when you should say no is really being mean. Saying no can be mean, but only if you say it out of your soul, out of selfish desires. You cannot say no with bitterness or hatred and be right. The right no must come by the Holy Spirit in boldness, delivered in the love of God.

God says no, as we saw earlier in this book. He began saying no in the garden of Eden, and no is still a major word in His vocabulary. God said no to Cain's offering. (See Genesis 4:1–7.) He said, "No, I will not receive your substitute offering."

And He did not. He did not back down from His no. God always has said no to sin and always will. He says no to wrong ideas that people have. He says no to anything that does not line up with His Word or His will. That is His right. He is called God for one good reason: He is God.

God said no to Satan when he attempted to take over the kingdom. Satan had said in his heart, *"I will exalt my throne above the stars of God"* (Isaiah 14:13). God said, "You will not do it," and then He kicked the devil out of his position of power and authority. (See Revelation 12:7–9.)

God did not hesitate. He did not discuss opinions or strategies or compromises with the devil, and He certainly did not call a summit of the spirit world. He did not say, "Let's have a committee meeting about this, and maybe we can share equal power."

God looked at Lucifer and said, "No, you will not. Out you go. Who do you think you are? Is the creation trying to be greater than the Creator?" He took action immediately with a very strong, loud, bold no. God did not ask Satan what he thought about the situation, either. He just declared, "Out!"

> **The right no must come by the Holy Spirit in boldness and the love of God.**

Was God mean when He said no to Lucifer? Of course not. With things as bad as they are in the world when God said no to the devil, I would hate to think where we would all be if God had let him do whatever he wanted!

Jesus said, *"I beheld Satan as lightning fall from heaven"* (Luke 10:18). When Satan fell, it was noticeable. If God says no, and you try to change that no to a yes, it will cause you to fall also.

CHAPTER
TWELVE

NO MEANS TAKING
A STAND

Another important fact you need to know about the anointed word *no* is that it will create enemies at times. You might as well get prepared for that. Many people are not used to hearing no in today's permissive society, and they do not like it when you use it. That is why a lot of people do not use the word more often—no one likes enemies. We all like to be liked. However, I would rather say no and be God's friend than not say it and have a group of losers for friends, wouldn't you?

NO MAKES ENEMIES

If you want to be God's friend, you must stand on the truth and declare no when it should be no, and yes when it should be yes. The Bible says that in the last days there will be those who hate Christians for His name's sake. Say no sometimes, and it is a guaranteed result that you will have enemies.

Remember, however, *"Greater is he that is in you, than he that is in the world"* (1 John 4:4), and *"No weapon that is formed against thee shall prosper"* (Isaiah 54:17).

A missionary friend of mine is alive today because she said no and then stood on God's Word. Late one night in a foreign country by herself, she was surrounded by ten men. Great fear attempted to engulf her because she is blonde and fair-skinned, and she knew those men were attracted by her looks and meant her no good.

Everything inside her was scream- **Stand on the** ing to run, she told me, but she knew **name of Jesus** there was no way she could outrun them **and declare a** all. She had to say no to what her soul **strong no. It will** was thinking and to the reactions of her **protect you.** flesh. The two Scripture verses quoted above rose up in her spirit, she said.

She pointed to one of the men and said loud, bold, and strong, "No, no you don't! Move out of my way. In Jesus' name, get out of my way. I am coming through."

At first, the men just stood there leering at her.

Then she pointed her finger and said, "In Jesus' name, move, NOW."

One man bowed to her and motioned her past, so she walked on through the men. When she got around the corner, she ran for her life!

No one protected her. She stood on the name of Jesus and on His Word and declared a strong no. The devil is out to destroy us, but if we rise up and boldly declare no to ungodly things, he cannot harm us. It is time the church rose up and declared her position.

In these last days, many will be deceived. The Bible says that even some of the elect will go astray. Why? They have not learned to say no. Those who are not deceived will be fought by those who are.

Saying no to their doctrines and to their operations causes some people to become your enemies. Some will not like you, and some may hate you. When you say no, some may fight you tooth and nail. But do not waver. Keep saying no, no, no. If God be for you, who can be against you?

NO HAS A BACKBONE

One of the things my grandmother used to say to me is, "Any old dead fish can float down the river, but it takes one with backbone to swim up the river against the current."

No is part of our spiritual backbone. God did not make us spineless jellyfish. He made us in His image, and God has a backbone. It does not take a backbone to go with the flow of people's ideas, thoughts, and opinions. If they are wrong, we need to realize we can say no.

Look at all the people to whom God said no: Lucifer, Adam and Eve, Cain, Samson, David, Saul, Eli, Samuel, Judas. God is not afraid to use the word *no,* and we should not be either. We are made in God's image, so that means we also can say no at the proper time and place. Through His Word, He teaches us when and how to say no.

In addition to accounts of those who did not say no at the proper time and place, the Bible gives stories of those who did: Noah, Abraham, Joseph, Joshua and Caleb, Daniel, and Esther in the Old Testament. In the New Testament, there is Joseph, Mary's husband, as well as the disciples Peter and John, and the apostle Paul.

CHAPTER THIRTEEN

WHEN TO SAY NO

There are a number of things to which God has told us to say no in His Word. Among these are devils, certain brothers in the Lord, evil, torment of the past, certain women, fools, and liars.

He said to have no fellowship with devils. (See 1 Corinthians 10:20.) How do you have fellowship with the devil? By accepting demons and allowing them to have influence in your life. *No* means absolutely no acceptance of that thing, that person, or that particular idea. *No* stops things from coming into existence in your life.

In 1 Corinthians 5:11, the Word warns us not even to eat with certain brothers.

But now I have written unto you not to keep company, if any man that is called a brother be a fornicator, or covetous, or an idolater, or a railer, or a drunkard, or an extortioner; with such an one no not to eat.

The Bible does not mince words here. Paul wrote very clearly not to even eat with these people. That does not mean to go over and try to save them. Yes, there are some cases where you may help someone, but in other cases, the Word is very explicit. Just say no.

Paul was not even talking about sinners here, but a brother. He was very explicit: Don't even eat with them!

Why was he so emphatic? He did not intend for the Corinthians to misunderstand him. If we get around people like that, the world begins to pull on us, as well as them. God wants us to say no to any fellowship with the devil.

LOVE THE PERSON, NOT HIS SIN

People say, "But it is not flesh and blood against which we war. It is principalities, powers, and wickedness in high places." (See Ephesians 6:12; 2 Corinthians 10:3–5.)

That is true. But guess who the wickedness comes through? People. So we need to avoid such people. You can continue to love the person in the name of Jesus, but if they do not change, you have to say no to them. Otherwise, you will be allowing whatever is in them to jump onto you, your family, your church, and so forth. Say no to whatever their sin is, and save the time and energy you would have spent fighting it off.

If you are going to love God, you must learn to hate evil with a passion.

The Bible says, *"Abhor that which is evil; cleave to that which is good"* (Romans 12:9), or "Say no to what is evil, and say yes to what is good." If you are going to love God, you must learn to hate evil with a passion. You must campaign against the evil of this world. Campaign in prayer. Protest personally against the works of the devil.

The Bible also says, *"Resist the devil, and he will flee from you"* (James 4:7). What does it mean to resist? It means to say no. Say, "No, devil," and he has to go roam somewhere else because *no* shuts every door and window and pulls down the blinds so the devil cannot even see inside. No is a glorious word that keeps the devil out.

SAY NO TO THE DEVIL'S REMINDERS

No shuts the door to the torment of being haunted by your past. At times, demons will take the past and try to torment or haunt us with it—especially if we have not asked forgiveness for something. Unforgiveness really opens the door to the devil's tricks. That is why it is so important to walk in love and to repent immediately when we do something we should not. (See Psalm 103:12 and Micah 7:19.)

The devil loves to remind you of past mistakes. In fact, he seems to deal more with the past than with anything else. If God has forgiven us and erased those sins or mistakes, then we need to leave them erased. Say no to the devil's haunting, and he has to flee. He will run from you if you say no. Keep saying no until he quits harassing and haunting you with that thing. Find a verse on which to stand. (See Romans 4:22-24.) *No* is like a razor. It sets you free.

Proverbs talks a lot about saying no. One proverb tells men to stay away from those women who "cry out in the streets" for you to come into their beds. The Word did not say for us to interview them to find out why they do what they do, or to take pictures and write articles and books about them.

I know one person who had a "street ministry to prostitutes and homosexuals." The next thing I knew, he was both! I know that is a wild statement, but it is the truth. The Word does not tell us to interview such people and get on their level in order "to relate better" to them. The Word says to tell them the good news, then go.

The Word also says, "Tell fools no." Proverbs 23:9 says that if you talk with a fool, he will despise the wisdom of your words. The only way you can deal with some people is just to say no and walk on without turning back. Also, Proverbs 19:22 tells us to say no to liars. Say, "No. I am not going to walk with you. You are a liar. Good-bye."

No is powerful. *No* will protect you. So why do people not use it more? For several reasons, but usually because they do not understand what no is.

CHAPTER
FOURTEEN

REASONS WHY PEOPLE DO NOT SAY NO

The first reason *no* is not used much anymore is that people are no longer accustomed to absolutes. As a proclaimer of the word *no,* you stand alone. In the world today, if no is said, it almost always is given with an excuse. It is not the absolute that it should be.

The soul does not like yes and no. They are "commitment" words. People are afraid of that today.

No is contagious. If it is used correctly, it will be a healthy contagiousness. What the church needs today is a *no* epidemic. We would be a lot healthier. The world says, "Whatever you want, it's okay. If it feels good, do it. Whatever makes you happy." We do not need that philosophy from the pit of hell in the church.

The second reason *no* is not popular is that it causes reactions. People do not always receive *no* in a nice way, nor with the acceptance we all crave. The primary reason people do not like to say no is because the reactions they often get are hard to cope with. Many times people will ask us, "Why?" But remember that *no* is an anointed word that does not need to be explained. In fact, most of the time, it should not be explained. By explaining, many times we lose the force of the declaration.

My grandmother, who helped with my upbringing, always said, "When I say no, it is no forever." There was no changing her mind, and that is the way it should be in the realm of the spirit. Somehow, today, our nos mean very little. It has been so watered down. Most of the time, it turns into a social yes, or a soulish yes. Either one will get you in big trouble.

> **This is how it should be: When we say no, it is no forever.**

NO ANGERS REBELLIOUS PEOPLE

No angers dominant or controlling people or those with self-will and rebellion. Watch for their reactions. People will come up with all sorts of excuses, reasons, and explanations to counteract your *no*. They will cry or get mad and yell. They will try all sorts of things to move you off your stand. Emotional manipulation comes into full manifestation when you start saying no to people who do not like the sound of that word.

One reaction to *no* is self-pity. I like helping poor people, but I refuse to help lazy people. You are not helping someone if you help them to "mooch." The Bible says that if you do not work, you are not to eat. (See 2 Thessalonians 3:10.) And the Word says if you do not feed your family, you are worse than an infidel. (See 1 Timothy 5:8.) That is a heavy statement, but it is true. I did not make it up. The Bible states it.

Therefore, watch out for professional beggars who make the church rounds. When you recognize them and say no, they may cry and begin emotional manipulation plays. If you are not careful, you will change your no to a yes. Self-pity is a common reaction to *no*. Self-pity always pleases the flesh of a person.

A third reason people do not say no is guilt. Often, people feel guilty at saying no, as if it were a dirty word or a bad word. It is so rarely used today that it sounds funny to our ears. I have learned to say no to people and go on about my business, not even thinking of the incident again. You have to learn to say no and walk away. You should not feel any guilt saying no when it should be said.

DO NOT HESITATE TO SAY NO

People motivated by mercy can be abused more than others because they find it so hard to say no. However, more than most people, they need to learn to say it, go home, and not feel guilty. People will run you ragged if you do not stop them. Demons will run you crazy if you do not stop them.

Suppose a friend calls with free tickets to a basketball game on an afternoon when the Lord has called you to pray. You find it so difficult to say no that you say, "Well, let me think about it." You know you should not go, but you waver and then give in and go. The next day you feel rotten because you know you should not have gone.

Even if you get the courage to call and cancel your plans, you feel guilty. What should have been a strong, positive *no* turned into a puny, miserable, guilty *no*. If you had said no in the first place, there would have been no guilt. All of us have fallen into this trap at one time or another.

A fourth reason why people do not say no more often is because they think it sounds mean. It sometimes sounds mean because the soul does not like to be told no. The soul likes its own way. If your child squirms away from you and runs toward the street where traffic is rushing by, you scream, "No!" Was that mean? Of course not. That *no* was the nicest thing you could say. It was protection for your child.

Suppose you have just gotten up in the morning and are beginning to pray. Your soul and body are saying, "Sleep, sleep. We need more sleep." They do not need more sleep. Say, "No, we are going to pray, so shut up." Is it mean to tell your body and soul no when your spirit knows it is far better to be praying? No, it is not mean. It is good.

I say no a lot. I know *no* is not mean, but not everyone else does yet. A lot of people call and want me to preach in their churches. I pray over the invitations I get. If God wants me to go, I say yes. If God tells me not to go, I say no.

A PERSONAL EXAMPLE

I have discovered that some people will not take no for an answer. They keep trying to get you to change your mind.

"But, Brother Liardon, you have to come to these meetings. They just will not be successful unless you come," they tell me.

I reply, "That is the problem. You do not want me or the gift of the Holy Spirit operating through me. You want to draw people. If the meeting will not be successful without my presence, it is not God. I am not coming. Thank you for asking me, but no, I am not coming. Good-bye."

I will not hold meetings to help someone draw crowds. I only go when the Lord says to go and when He has something

He wants said to those people. That should be the only reason for anyone to have a meeting. The people may say, "Please, Brother Liardon. We will guarantee you all this money." But I still say no. My answer is no forever unless God tells me otherwise. Money cannot buy me.

A certain pastor who had a tendency to be "pushy" called my office one time and hassled one of the men who works for me. He wanted this staff member to give him my phone number so that he could discuss my holding a meeting for him.

My worker replied, "He is out on a trip right now. If you will give us your name and number, we will pass it on to him, and he will get back to you."

The pastor persisted, "Well, where is he? I will call him myself."

Our ministry policy does not permit that, and my staff know it. My staff member said, "We don't like to disturb him during a meeting. We'll call him and give him your name and number. Then he will call you when he can. Otherwise, you can call him when he returns." Then this pastor yelled at the man who works for me. He not only yelled, but he also swore at him.

The man who works for me has wisdom. He did not yell back. He did not even tell me what had happened until some time later. But one day we were looking over our invitations, praying about them, and working out a schedule for the future. We came to this pastor's invitation, and I asked my staff member about it. He still did not tell me what happened, but his voice was not right. I know my people, and I know their voices. (You need to know your family like that. Then you can help them in time of trouble and they can help you.)

I said, "Your voice does not sound right. What is the problem here?"

Then he told me what this pastor had done.

"Lose his phone number forever!" I instructed my worker.

Eventually, that pastor called again and started the whole routine, "You must come to our church. You are such a gift to the body—"

I said, "Sir, would you be quiet for a moment? I want to talk to you, and I want you to know why I am doing what I am doing. I don't want any confusion here. I want you to understand me clearly.

"First of all, I am glad you called. I am glad you like my ministry and that you have read my books. That is very nice.

"But *I will not preach in your church.* Not now, not ever—unless God specifically tells me otherwise. You have treated one of the people who works for me badly. You even cursed him. When you do something like that to one of my people, you have done it to me. And when you have done it to them or to me, you have done it to Jesus."

He began to sputter, whine, and try to explain away his actions.

But I said, "My answer to your invitation is no, unless God hits me on the side of the head and tells me to go to your church. You can call. You can fuss. You can criticize. You can backbite me or stab me in the back all you want, but my answer is still no.

"Let me say again, however, that I want you to know why I am taking this stand. You are supposed to be a man of God.

You are older than I, and I think someone who has been in the ministry as long as you have would have enough self-control not to curse."

He apologized, but that did not change my answer.

CHAPTER

FIFTEEN

FIVE NO FACTS

R ememembering these five facts about saying no will help you to say no and protect your destiny.

1. *No* **is one of the words people most wish they had said in past situations.**

A young lady who graduated from high school with me is an example. She is now in her early twenties, divorced, and a mother. All because she did not say no one night to her boyfriend.

People are pastoring wrong churches because they did not say no.

Some Christians have lost their rewards or crowns in heaven because they did not say no at the right time.

2. *No* **originated in heaven with God.**

Yes and no are appropriate responses to right and wrong. God originated these responses.

3. *No* **protects you and stops the devil.**

No would have protected the young lady I mentioned above, and her entire life would have been different.

4. *No* is a part of the teachings of the Bible.

We have already discussed a number of people from the Bible who said yes when they should have said no, or vice versa. The consequences of their actions are plainly written out for all who will read them to profit by this example.

5. *No* can be said by anyone.

You do not have to be fifty years old in the Lord before you can say no. You can be five seconds old in Jesus and say no. Anyone can say no.

Learning to say no is so important to our destinies. That's why, when God says no through us, it is anointed.

Just say no.

CHAPTER
16
SIXTEEN

NO AFFECTS DESTINIES

God told Noah to build an ark. Noah built it, but not without opposition. The entire time he was constructing the ark, his countrymen were making jokes at his expense and criticizing him. However, Noah said no to men and yes to God. After he built the ark, Noah and his family climbed in. Can you imagine the reaction from his neighbors?

"What are you doing in there, Noah? Hey Noah, where is the rain? It is not raining yet, you crazy nut. As a matter of fact, it has never rained! What are you going to do with this ark-thing anyhow? Come on out, Noah. Nothing is going to happen."

What did Noah do? He obeyed God and said no to those people. It is a good thing that he did, or where would we be today? *No* affects destinies, sometimes of many people. When you say no, it is not just your own life at stake. Your no may affect hundreds or thousands of people.

An example of this kind of *no* is shown in the life of Abraham. When God told him to leave his own country, Abraham had a decision to make: to obey God or stay where he was.

(See Genesis 12:1–4.) I am certain that Abraham's relatives and friends thought he was crazy. They probably let him know it, too. There was no doubt a strong pull on him to remain in the land he knew so well with all the comforts, position, and conveniences that he had. But Abraham said no to the flesh and to other people and yes to God.

Abraham also said no to strife with Lot. It is too bad Lot did not learn from his uncle how important that little word was. It would have saved him a lot of trouble and heartache. Abraham's great-grandson Joseph knew this. He said no to the temptations of Potiphar's wife. (See Genesis 39:6–15.) No doubt she was one of the most beautiful women in the country, but Joseph refused her.

NO MAY NOT LOOK SMART

At first, it did not look like a smart move. In the long run, however, Joseph's no saved many lives, not just the lives of the Israelites but the lives of many Egyptians who would have starved during the famine that came later.

Your no also may affect many lives.

Say no to fears and doubts, and your no may affect many lives.

Look at Joshua and Caleb, as reported in Numbers 13 and 14. The other ten spies sent into Israel to report on the land brought back an evil report. Joshua and Caleb stood up and said no to the evil report and the taunts of the people.

But notice who went in to possess the land. Those who said yes to their flesh and to fears and doubts never saw the promised land. If we say yes to the devil's crowd, we will never enter into the promises and victories that are ours.

151

Another example of someone who said no was Daniel. He said no to the king's edict not to pray in any other name but the king's. Instead, Daniel obeyed God. He opened his windows and prayed so that everyone could hear him. (See Daniel 6:10.) Daniel was not afraid to say no, and the entire kingdom was turned around because Daniel did what was right in the sight of God. That took a backbone of steel. He knew the consequence would be the lions' den, but he still said no.

Daniel's fellow countrymen Shadrach, Meshach, and Abednego also said no to the king of Babylon. (See Daniel 3.) They refused to bow down and worship false idols. Their *no* was unshakable. The king said he would throw them in the fiery furnace if they continued to say no. They did not waver or budge an inch. "No, no, no," they replied.

The king threw them in the fiery furnace just as he said he would, and the three young men were engulfed by the flames. Then one of the greatest miracles ever reported took place. In front of everyone's eyes, a fourth man appeared in the flames! Say no to the devil and his crowd, and you will see miracles, also. However, you will not see miracles happening in an atmosphere that is not right. If God says no, and man says yes, you had better agree with God.

SAY NO TO THE DEVIL

Esther and her kinsman Mordecai give us two more examples of those who stood up and said no in the face of tremendous opposition. Esther went uninvited to her husband, the king, knowing it might cost her life. (See Esther 5:1–4.) King Ahasuerus honored the man named Haman and his plot to destroy the Jews. But Mordecai said no and would not kneel down to Haman or pay him honor. (See Esther 3:2.) Mordecai persuaded Esther also to say no, and the Jewish people of that day were saved. You can be sure all of those people were glad Mordecai and Esther stood up for God and said no to man.

In the New Testament, Joseph is a man who affected the destinies of multitudes of people by saying no. In that day, if a woman became pregnant before marriage, she was liable to be stoned. When Joseph found that Mary was pregnant and knew he was not the father, he had every right to turn her over to the authorities. But he did not. He said no to cultural and religious tradition and said yes to God. (See Matthew 1:18–25.) What if Joseph had not said no to men and yes to God?

Time and time again throughout both the Old and New Testaments, we can see the results that a good, strong, bold, powerful *No!* can produce.

King Herod ordered the magi to go to Bethlehem, locate the baby, and then report back to him in Jerusalem. The magi went to Bethlehem, but that is as far as their yes went. They said no to King Herod, and although they knew exactly where Jesus was, they never did report back to Herod. (See Matthew 2:12.)

Many of the miracles in the New Testament would not have happened if people had not said no. Mary Magdalene said no to the jeers and leers of those who said she should not go near Jesus. She said no to people and yes to God and was totally set free. She became one of Jesus' most faithful followers.

SAY NO TO TRADITION

The woman with the issue of blood should never have been out in public. She had been hemorrhaging for twelve years. During that time, she must have been kept separate from the people because it was against the statutes of Israel to be among people if you were bleeding. Blood meant that you were unclean.

This woman knew that to go out in public and try to get to Jesus meant certain stoning and death. She did not care anymore what people thought of her. She said no to people's opinion and to tradition and did everything she could to receive her miracle. Her *no* to the world brought her into contact with Jesus, and she was totally healed.

Another woman who said no said it to Jesus! She had come to Him on behalf of her daughter who was demon possessed. (See Matthew 15:22–28.) Jesus told her that He was only sent to the lost sheep of Israel and that it was not right to take the children's bread and toss it to the dogs. The woman could have hung her head and crawled away, but she did not. She said no to the traditional religious barriers involved and stood up for her miracle. Jesus respected her faith and freed her daughter from bondage.

Peter and John knew the value of *no*. In Acts 4, the religious leaders commanded them not to preach Christ any longer. But the apostles said, "No. We must obey God rather than you." Then they went out and did exactly what they had been told by man not to do. Mighty miracles occurred in their ministries. Notice what they said:

> *And now, Lord, behold their threatenings: and grant unto thy servants, that with all boldness they may speak thy word, by stretching forth thine hand to heal; and that signs and wonders may be done by the name of thy holy child Jesus. And when they had prayed, the place was shaken where they were assembled together; and they were all filled*

*with the Holy Ghost, and they spake the word of God with
boldness.* (Acts 4:29–31)

Right after this, the story is told of two people who lied
to Peter in the presence of the Holy Spirit and dropped dead.
Unlike Peter and John, Ananias and Sapphira said yes to the
world and lost everything. (See Acts 5:1–16.) From then on,
Peter and John went out boldly performing miracles. They
knew how to say no to man and yes to God.

PAUL SAID NO MANY TIMES

Another man in the Bible, Paul, seemed to love the word
no. When political or religious leaders tried to keep him from
preaching, he said no. He was thrown into prison, beaten,
robbed, and left for dead at various times. He could easily
have decided the ministry was too tough and quit. But he did
not. Paul said, *"I am not ashamed of the gospel of Christ"* (Romans
1:16), and *"for me to live is Christ, and to die is gain"* (Philippians
1:21).

There were probably plenty of opportunities for Paul to
give up and go on to be with the Lord. But he said, "No, I will
press on," and he did.

Paul was never one to mince words. His yes was yes, and
his no was no. He may have had few close friends, but he certainly was God's close friend. Why? Paul knew when to say
yes and when to say no. Half the New Testament was written
by Paul. If you read his epistles very closely, you will find *no* in
them over and over again. He knew the importance of saying
no.

If Paul were alive today, he would more than likely look
you in the eye and exclaim, *"Just say no!"*

HOW TO
SURVIVE
AN ATTACK

CONTENTS

HOW TO SURVIVE AN ATTACK

1. Know Your Enemy 161
2. How to Recognize an Attack 166
3. How to Go through an Attack.................................. 181
4. The Soul under Attack..201
5. The Will under Attack 206
6. The Emotions under Attack.....................................219
7. The Intellect under Attack 226
8. The Imagination under Attack.................................233
9. The Memory under Attack 240
10. The Human Body under Attack...............................248
11. The Human Spirit under Attack 254
12. The Recovery Zone 260

CHAPTER

1

ONE

KNOW YOUR ENEMY

It was three o'clock in the morning. My room was dark and wonderfully quiet, and I was doing what most people should be doing at that particular hour—sleeping!

I had just returned from an exhausting schedule of ministry. The meetings had been good, and lives were changed. I was happy and at peace. Everything was calm and in order, and I was totally relaxed, enjoying my rest.

But things were about to change.

All of a sudden, the shrill ringing of my telephone pierced the night and abruptly ended my moment of comfort. I fumbled for the telephone receiver, and from the other end a frantic voice whined, "Roberts! Roberts! Help me...help me."

As I listened to the circumstances of my distraught friend, I interrupted and said, "You are not seeing clearly. This is not a problem—it's the devil."

"The devil?" He was shocked.

"That's right. It's the devil. You are under attack and don't even know it."

As I continued to talk with him into the wee hours of the morning, I began to realize that many Christians do not know the tactics of their enemy. They may be good, faithful people, filled with the love and zeal of God, and still be totally ignorant when it comes to the schemes of the devil.

As believers, we should not be afraid to discuss the devil. Jesus mentioned and taught about him often in the New Testament. Jesus did not exalt the devil by discussing him. He *exposed* him by teaching the disciples about his devices.

Understand this principle: Exposing the devil is not our priority; *knowing God is.* But anything that hinders our relationship with God or attempts to abort His plan in the earth must be dealt with and properly understood.

On one hand, Jesus came and taught the truth about God, exposing the lies the enemy had perpetrated against Him. On the other hand, He dealt openly with the devil and his demons and taught the people their authority over him.

Anything that hinders our relationship with God must be dealt with.

The apostle Paul wrote in 2 Corinthians 2:11, *"Lest Satan should get an advantage of us: for we are not ignorant of his devices."*

We have a mandate, a commission from God, to know our enemy. If we as believers do not understand or comprehend his tactics, then the Bible says he will get an advantage over us. If we do not know the way our enemy operates, then he will have the ability to deceive us and cause us to waste our lives.

We who are born again have been purchased by the blood of Jesus. As believers, it is true that we enter into the benefits of the finished works of Christ, but nowhere does Scripture teach that the new birth automatically eliminates demonic *influence* or demonic *attack*. Jesus personally dealt with the enemy in the wilderness (see Luke 4) and throughout His public ministry as well.

As they walked with Jesus, the disciples also had to stand against the schemes of the devil in their own lives. Peter attempted to persuade Jesus not to go to the cross in Matthew 16:20–22. And although Peter vowed undying loyalty, Jesus told him he would deny Him three times, which Peter did. (See Matthew 26:33–34, 74.) Demonic power influenced one of the disciples to betray Him. (See Matthew 26:21–25.) When James and John did not like the actions of the Samaritans, Jesus rebuked

> **Lack of knowledge has caused many believers to fall and fail.**

them and told them, *"Ye know not what manner of spirit ye are of"* (Luke 9:55). Demonic influence and attack will attempt to come and persuade, no matter what level of maturity we walk in.

The first part of Hosea 4:6 states, *"My people are destroyed for lack of knowledge."*

Lack of knowledge in the area of demonic influence has caused many believers to fall and fail. Many open the trapdoors of calamity, destruction, and even death by not knowing the intention of their enemy. Part of the last commission Jesus gave us before He left the earth was, *"In my name shall they cast out devils"* (Mark 16:17).

We cannot cast out something we do not know or understand. Ignorance makes us immobile. It causes us to remain passive in an area because we do not understand it. Ignorance gives ground and entrance to the schemes of the devil. Ignorance works for the enemy because it gives him freedom to pursue and conquer without being noticed.

When we do not properly discern the schemes of the enemy, it will negatively affect our churches, our nation, and every other sphere of our lives. *We must preach and know the whole gospel, not just a part of it.* When we refuse to recognize our enemy, we become prey to him. When we shrink away from truth and refuse to examine it or learn from it, then we remain unprepared for the attacks of a raging enemy.

The Bible is not ashamed to discuss and expose the devil. From Genesis to Revelation, the entire plan and purpose of our enemy unfolds. It is our responsibility to train and mature ourselves through the Word, prayer, the leading of the Holy Spirit, and the godly authority that God has positioned over us.

Because some believers fail to take the responsibility of maturing themselves, the plan of God is thwarted in their lives. As a result, some are trying to live in the midst of an attack and cannot see nor understand why they act the way they do or think the way they may think. They think instead it is just their personality or their circumstances.

I am not saying that every negative situation we face is caused by a demon, because I don't believe it is. Many times we find ourselves in trouble because of undisciplined flesh and desires. We are not dealing with that side in this book. Understand that trouble comes several ways, two being *uncontrolled flesh* and *demonic influence.* The purpose of this book, however, is to enlighten our walk as believers regarding the attacks of the enemy.

The Word of God was written for our instruction, to teach and train us. Written on the pages of the Bible are truths of life, health, and peace. If we fall, through those truths we can stand again. Through embracing those truths, we are healed if sickness comes. As we mature our inner man through prayer and the Word, we don't have to fall prey to deception. If we embrace the Word of God as our safeguard, we can effectively stand, prevail, and conquer when an attack comes. Jesus said it in John 10:10; *believe it.* Through Him, we can have life, and life more abundantly!

CHAPTER

TWO

HOW TO RECOGNIZE AN ATTACK

In the natural realm of life, we have several different branches of the military that train and equip themselves to do battle. These men and women undergo extensive drills to learn the strategy of their enemy. Not only do they train themselves in expertise with their weaponry, but they also learn the methods for an attack and the situations that are conducive to one. They are trained to be loyal and committed to protect their boundary. They know the importance of unity in winning a battle. They are drilled in diligence and skill for the sake of their nation and loved ones.

The discipline they undergo in training pays off when a surprise attack comes. The months they spend awakened at the crack of dawn and the repeated examination of their weapons enable them to respond without much thought. The constant drill places a *habit* inside of them, *not a formula*. The weeks of crawling through a field on their chest with live bullets flying overhead causes them to face obstacles despite fear. They are trained and equipped.

Thus, this trained military develops a bond with their weapons. They would not think of approaching enemy territory without them. Picture it. A soldier unarmed would be a joke! They know where a land mine is probable; they can detect an approaching enemy; they know when to take cover and when to attack. The military is secure because of its preparation and insight. It is easy to recognize an attack. You can hear the bombs explode, the torpedoes drop, and the machine guns fire.

An attack in the spirit can be recognized in the same way. The problem is, we have not taken the time to train ourselves, so we turn a deaf ear to the evidence of the enemy. Then we wake up and wonder why we are in the condition we're in!

> **We should know before the battle starts that the devil is attacking.**

The sad thing is, when the battle is over, it is easy to say, "That was the devil." As believers, we should know *before* the battle ever starts that it is the devil. Just as soldiers in the military have been trained for conflict, we must train for spiritual conflict.

GODLY CONFRONTATION

We don't just wake up one day and our homes have fallen apart. We don't just look around and our children have run away from home. We don't just get up some morning and find we are in total poverty. It starts someplace. The first time you felt an impression that something was not right, what did you do? *Did you ignore it or confront it?*

When we ignore a bad situation, it will continue to worsen. The devil won't go away if we leave him an open door. Uncontrolled desires will not disappear. Ignoring destructive situations will cause the downfall of our family, our health, and our circumstances.

Let us build within us the ability of godly confrontation. Godly confrontation results from a mature inner man, seasoned by the Word of God. Sometimes, when we hear the word *confront,* we think of loud aggression. I'm not talking about brash, rude confronting. I'm speaking of the confrontation that destroys the yoke of bondage.

Sometimes confronting comes by a soft answer. Sometimes the evil plans are confronted by an action—a counteraction by good. And yes, sometimes confrontation is loud. There are times when a person has been led so far by the enemy that he must be jerked back into reality. But always remember, whatever way the Holy Spirit leads you to confront, *godly results are produced.* A soft answer, a counteraction, or a loud confrontation are all direct and productive when you are led by God. They are *all* works of boldness. Jesus was the meekest man on earth; but He was not weak. He never failed to confront the works of the devil. He spoke the truth, but His methods of presentation were according to each circumstance.

> **When the Holy Spirit leads you to confront, godly results are produced.**

TEST THE SOURCE

Don't believe the lie, "Well, some things happen for the glory of God." God does not redeem us from something and then test us with it. He doesn't put sickness, disease, death, or poverty on us to teach humility. He will not cause us to go through something He paid for at the cross. So many talk doubt and unbelief, giving glory to the enemy while thinking they are being humble for God.

The enemy will come and whisper, "You are an unworthy soul." You might say, "That's right." Then he'll say, "God is going to teach you something through sickness and disease." Again you respond, "That's right." The next thing you know, we're burying you!

We must know the character of God to recognize an attack. If we really know who God is and how He operates, then we will be able to detect and destroy the devices of the enemy.

The Bible says in John 10:10,

The thief cometh not, but for to steal, and to kill, and to destroy: I am come that they might have life, and that they might have it more abundantly.

If we have lessons to learn, then learn them through prayer, the Word, and godly leadership. Why suffer under the hand of the enemy, blame God, and then if you live through it, say you've learned something?

TEMPTATION AND WILES

The devil plans his attack. He has a strategy in every situation. The first step in recognizing an attack is understanding the devil will work his strategy in one of two ways: by wiles or temptations.

Temptations are obvious. They are outright, blatant words, exposures, or situations. The Bible says in James 1:14 that we can only fall into temptation through our own lusts that we have not dealt with. Understand that God does not tempt you. (See

James 1:13.) The enemy will use a temptation against you in an area that has caused you trouble in the past. Temptation comes as a way the enemy plans to abort you from the will of God. It is an attack designed to make you to sin, to harden your heart against the Spirit of the Lord.

Temptations can cause heaviness and depression. Sometimes they come in manifold numbers. But those who trust in the Lord at these times are safe and secure. Second Peter 2:9 says, *"The Lord knoweth how to deliver the godly out of temptations."*

The Bible says that every man is tempted. Hebrews 4:15 says Jesus Himself *"was in all points tempted like as we are, yet without sin."* His identification with us and His death on the cross paid for our freedom from the clutches of temptation.

Christ's death on the cross paid for our freedom from temptation.

The second strategy of the devil is through the means of a *wile. A wile is a scheme that is hidden to deceive. It is not obvious like a temptation.* A wile intends to lure you as if by a magic spell. It craftily covers itself to lead you into deception.

Although the Bible only uses the word *wiles* once in the New Testament, Scripture repeatedly warns us of deceptions. The Bible is clear when Scripture speaks of deception. Those who have embraced a wile are deceived when:

- They are only a hearer of the Word and not a doer. (See James 1:22.)

- They think they have no sin. (See 1 John 1:8.)

- They think they are something when they are nothing. (See Galatians 6:3.)

- They think they are wise with the wisdom of the world. (See 1 Corinthians 3:18.)

- They have an unbridled tongue yet they consider themselves religious. (See James 1:26.)

- They think they can sow and not reap what they've sown. (See Galatians 6:7.)

- They think the unrighteous can inherit the kingdom of God. (See 1 Corinthians 6:9.)

- They think contact and communion with sin will not have an effect on them. (See 1 Corinthians 15:33.)

- They think they can lie, have no remorse for sin, and not depart from the faith. (See 1 Timothy 4:1–3.)

Truth is the only antidote for deception. We can be alerted to every scheme if we will listen to our spirits. We may not understand it completely, but we should back away until we do. Then we also judge everything by the truth of the Scripture and the character of God. Those two safeguards will ground an enemy missile every time.

> **Truth is the only antidote for deception.**

DEMONIC RANK

Another way to recognize an attack is to discern the level of our enemy. Just as we mentioned before, the devil has rank, order, and governments in his kingdom. It is important that we know what they are.

In Ephesians 6:12, the apostle Paul categorized the ranks of evil spirits. He said,

For we wrestle not against flesh and blood, but against principalities, against powers, against the rulers of the

darkness of this world, against spiritual wickedness in high places.

Every evil spirit has an assigned position. To recognize the level of attack, we must see each spirit's sphere of influence.

Principalities are the force and dominion that deal with nations and governments. That is their regime. The order of the government in a nation and the economy of the world can be influenced by these principalities.

Powers have authority and power to take action in any sphere that is open to them. Wherever entrance is given that will affect a multitude, the work of an evil power will be searching for an opening.

World rulers are evil spirits that govern the darkness and blindness of the world, keeping people from seeing the wickedness and deception they are in.

Wicked spirits operate from heavenly places. Their target is the church, and their method is wiles and deceptions. Fiery darts, onslaughts, doctrines of devils, and every false work represent deceptions they are capable of carrying out.

There are also demons that are of a low degree. To be honest with you, these spirits are dumb. They scream, holler, harass, aggravate, and mean absolutely nothing. They have a little bit of power, but they can only bother us if we fear them.

The high-ranking spirits are very smart, and they watch. They watch what you say, they watch where you look, and they watch where you go. Then, just as our natural military does, they go back with their information and plan a strategy against you. Their purpose is to destroy you and the church.

These spirits are one reason why great ministries have fallen. A high-level strategy attack was implemented against them, and it was not recognized until it was too late. We will never recognize an attack of the enemy unless we learn his methods.

SYMPTOMS OF AN ATTACK

The enemy will attack you in the realms of your mind, your body, and your spirit. I will discuss these areas in the chapters to come. But before we discuss those areas in detail, there are some basic signals we need to be alerted to.

Just as physical appetite leaves a person who is sick in their body, it is also the first thing to hit and leave a person who is under spiritual attack. They are not hungry for the things of God. They don't want to go to church, they don't want to pray, they don't want to read their Bible, and to be blunt, they don't really care about God at that moment. They like Him; but He's more like number four instead of number one in their lives.

> **People under attack place God at number four instead of number one in their lives.**

1. When a person is under attack, he may lose his spiritual hunger for God.

Since our spiritual hunger is the first thing the enemy will attack in us, we must protect it at all costs. Matthew 5:6 says, *"Blessed are they which do hunger and thirst after righteousness: for they shall be filled."*

If we do not hunger and thirst for the things of God and His character, there will be no infilling. An empty vessel will be filled with something—good or evil. Choose to protect what is of God and build upon it with the Word. Even when you might not feel like reading the Bible, pick it up and read it anyway!

The Bible is alive even when you feel dead. The written Word of God is one of your weapons of warfare. Learn to pull it out and feed yourself to sustain the life inside of you. The natural military does not always feel like pulling out their rifles, taking them apart, cleaning them, and putting them back together. But they know and understand that this weapon will save their lives in combat. The same is true for the written Word of God. You may not always feel like taking it out, reading it, and letting it adjust and cleanse you; but it will be your shield and buckler in spiritual combat.

When your desire for God leaves, it gives entrance to the enemy.

Have you ever seen a person who was really on fire for God get hit by the enemy and fade away? How could someone with so much zeal now be so backslidden?

Did you ever see someone expressive and free in praise and worship suddenly become still and cold?

The enemy has won over their hunger and desire for God, and now they have no motivation. Spiritual hunger is motivation to go on with God, just as physical hunger motivates you to eat. Spiritual hunger is an acquired taste. It sustains life.

People who are alcoholics have acquired the taste. There is no way a person can initially like alcohol. They trick themselves to continue drinking it until they acquire the taste and desire for it. They have become addicted and cannot live without it.

Spiritual hunger is an acquired desire and taste as well.

How do you become spiritually hungry? How do you stay spiritually hungry? It's simple. It's not always easy, but it's simple. You walk your bedroom floor and make yourself get hungry for God. You say out of your mouth, "I want more of You, God." Even when your mind says, "No, you don't," you say, "Yes, I do. Be quiet." You have to learn to talk to yourself and tell yourself how to think. That is how you take control of your mind and teach it to flow with the Word of God.

God cannot use someone who is divided within himself. If your mind is thinking of cooking the evening meal and your body is busy with something else, then the whole time you are praying, it is a divided prayer. *A fervent prayer that produces results is one prayed by someone whose mind agrees with his spirit, whose body is subdued, and whose spirit leads them both.* You have got to be together: spirit, mind, and body. That kind of prayer will see results. That is the effectual prayer of a righteous man.

It's not always easy, but it's simple to stay spiritually hungry.

When you are under the attack of the devil, you must make yourself hungry for the things of God. Think about the time you were sick and you did not want to eat. What did someone who cared about you say? They put food in front of you and said, "You need to eat this."

You probably said, "I don't want to eat it. I'm not hungry."

They said, "I don't care. Eat it." Why? Because they knew the nutrients in the food would strengthen your body and help it to overcome weakness. It will help you receive strength to overcome your illness.

When the body is sick, every part of the body is focused on the attack inside of it. To win in the spirit, the focus must be the same. When you are under attack, all of your energy must come from the strength you have built in the Lord to overcome it. You must keep your strength up and not grow weak.

When you are under the fire of the devil, that is not the time to quit going to church. That is not the time to quit reading the Word of God and confessing and praying. That is not the time to stop your labor for God. Instead, that is the time to turn it up!

Understand that the goal of the enemy is to rid you of spiritual desire for God. If you give in to it, you'll go under. It is only your Word level, your prayer level, and people of like faith that cause you to go over. You've got to stay around people who give you life when you are in a war. Don't hang around "deadbeats." Don't you know what I mean by that? Don't hang around lifeless, negative, carnal people.

> **The goal of the enemy is to rid you of spiritual desire for God.**

Above all, don't isolate yourself. Find someone who's "perking." Find someone with spunk and zeal for God. Their influence will help you and strengthen you in a time of trouble. The Bible says a good friend will sharpen you. (See Proverbs 27:17.)

2. The second thing that happens to a person under attack is a loss of strength.

Even though they smile and say the same things, they have lost that force about them. They don't have what I call the "bam!" in them. They have lost their spiritual punch and accuracy. There is no life, joy, or jump in them.

In Ephesians 6:10, Paul said, *"Finally, my brethren, be strong in the Lord, and in the power of his might."*

True joy, strength, and life come from the inward man. The only way you can effectively fight an attack is by gaining your strength from the Lord. *You cannot win outside of the spirit.* Allow your confession in the Word of God to give you strength: *"Let the weak say, **I am strong"** (Joel 3:10, emphasis added).

We must be careful not to rely on natural ability when we are in a spiritual war. When we are more comfortable with soulish and natural strengths than we are spiritual strengths, we end up helping the enemy. That is why sometimes, in a churchwide battle, there are disastrous splits and calamity, because believers go from spiritual combat into natural combat. They fall prey to mental ability. Natural combat uses its strength in cutting and slanderous words. Gossip and fear are its weapons.

We must learn to recognize the attack of the enemy in the area of spiritual strength. We must learn to stand and fight with the Word of God and in the realm of the Spirit. If we can remain in the Spirit and gain our strength from the Lord, the results will not be as disastrous.

3. The third way to recognize an attack is that you don't feel like yourself.

When the natural body is sick, we feel terrible. We have a tendency to be short with people. We usually act gripey and bossy even to those we love the most. We don't feel like ourselves; we feel strange and we act strange. When the body is sick, our natural tendency is to lay on the sofa, watch television, or go to bed and sleep the day away.

Learn to recognize a spiritual attack in the same way. When the enemy is attacking you, whether it is totally demonic or maneuvered through a human being, you begin to feel things that are not true. One of those feelings is paranoia. Do you know what I mean by that? You begin to feel like you are being judged and criticized, and that everyone is looking at you and telling you how awfully wrong you are. You feel like you can never please anyone because your life is such a spectacle. If you give in to those feelings, you'll quit and go backward. That is called an attack of the devil.

When those feelings come to you, learn how to reject them. You must learn to stand, resist, and fight back! Do not give in to them, retreat, and say, "Well, I must just be this way. I'll never do anything for God because I am no good." If you say that, the enemy has won.

I used to go through wars, and it would take me a while to figure out what I was in. I just thought, "Lord, I'm tired." I wanted to retreat, sit at home, and watch television. The saddest thing you can do when you are in a spiritual war is to watch secular television. Television is not wrong, but at that particular time in your life, it will feed your soul junk food instead of bread and dominate your spirit. The next worst thing you can do is go to bed and pretend the world doesn't exist. Your soul will sometimes "tilt" in spiritual warfare, so it will want to sleep and not deal with the reality around it. But the truth is, when you wake up, the enemy is still there and has possibly gained strength because you refused to fight.

You must learn to stand, resist, and fight back!

I had to learn that a war is made up of many battles, both great and small.

It was hard to pray during those times. As a matter of fact, I would have rather washed dishes than pray! I would say, "God, I don't want to deal with this. Just let me sit and do nothing. Please." Spiritual warfare drains your physical body. You don't want to talk; you don't want to eat. You don't want to see anyone, go anywhere, or do anything. It almost feels like someone has physically beat you up because that's what is happening in the spirit realm.

When people are in the spirit, they are outgoing. When people are flowing with God and secure in God, they have a joy that just won't end. *Love and joy come as a way of life when we live in the Spirit.* These people are strong, energetic, and aggressive. They focus on their purpose in the Spirit.

I had to learn that when I was in a war, I could not go to a place where there was no battle going on. That was retreat. There are no retreats in the kingdom of God. There are only charges! When you build your strength in God, you'll have that "charge" no matter what is happening around you.

> **Love and joy are a way of life when we live in the Spirit.**

When you are under fire, you bring out the biggest spiritual gun you have and blow that attack out of its arena. Many times when I am preaching, I can feel myself hit the war zone. Sometimes I stand up behind the pulpit and, before I've even said a word, I've already entered into it!

Don't ever be intimidated in a spiritual war. Intimidation is a major weapon of the enemy. Intimidation puts you in a box, and you can't come out and be yourself. The devil will try to make you feel insecure because anointed preaching exposes him for what he is. The enemy hates anointing. He hates those who know how to walk in it and administer it. The anointing breaks his yoke, his bondage, and his chains. It destroys the lies he has caused people to believe. When those bondages are broken, the people are set free and made strong. They don't take any more garbage from the devil, and he hates that.

One of the best tactics the enemy can use on a minister is to make him feel rejected, intimidated, and insecure. Why? Because it hinders him from speaking the truth that sets men free. God wants you to be yourself, seasoned with His Word. You are the victor, so be it. You are more than a conqueror; so conquer. Don't stand there and say, "Well, no one likes me." Say, "Devil, I break your power!"

The Bible calls the church an army, and that's not a nice little illustration! The Bible tells us that, because we are an army, we must learn the strategies of the enemy to conquer them. Learn to recognize when an attack comes, stand up to it, and win in the strength of the Lord.

CHAPTER

3

THREE

HOW TO GO THROUGH AN ATTACK

We have now established that we have an enemy. We have also learned the first warnings that come with a spiritual attack. You might have said, "That described me." Once we determine we are in an attack, we need to know how to win in it.

Understand that spiritual attacks will not go away by themselves. You cannot ignore the situation or pretend it does not exist. You cannot involve yourself in some other outlet and hope it will leave you alone if you don't think about it. We must not only learn how to stand against it but also how to *go through it* in total victory.

Before we can effectively win in an attack, there are some basic things we must realize.

NOT THE PERSON

In Ephesians 6:12 Paul told us,

For we wrestle not against flesh and blood, but against principalities, against powers, against the rulers of the darkness of this world, against spiritual wickedness in high places.

First of all, you must realize in your heart that *you are not fighting a person.* If you fall for the lie that you are fighting a natural person or problem during a spiritual attack, you will revert to natural means. *You will not win if you choose the road of gossip, slander, or revenge. You cannot have soulish discussion to ease spiritual pressure.*

Spiritual warfare means a spiritual influence over someone or something. The enemy might exercise control through another person; but it will hardly ever be through the same person he previously used. That can only happen if someone is still ignorant or open in this area of their life. We will discuss this area in a later chapter, but we must receive the basics of this principle first. Don't look at the persons who are causing you problems. Look beyond them to the true enemy.

If the devil cannot win over you through one person, he will wait awhile and try for one who is closer to you. He did the same with Jesus. The enemy attacked the ministry of Jesus through the multitudes and the religious leaders of the day. When He remained unmoved, the devil tried for the disciples. He tried through Peter and several others, but he succeeded in conquering Judas. Even though the attack came through someone close to Him, Jesus knew the source and remained unhindered. He knew His mission, and He kept His eyes on the goal of it. Even on the cross, He said, *"Father, forgive them; for they know not what they do"* (Luke 23:34).

> **Know your mission and keep your eyes on the goal.**

How could He say that? He was showing us a basic principle in surviving an attack. *Jesus was not interrupted by betrayal.* Forgiveness destroys the schemes of the devil. Forgiveness is a force that proves you know your God *and* your enemy. That is why Paul said,

> *To whom ye forgive any thing, I forgive also: for if I forgave any thing, to whom I forgave it, for your sakes forgave I it in the person of Christ; lest Satan should get an advantage of us: for we are not ignorant of his devices.*
>
> (2 Corinthians 2:10–11)

Forgiveness puts your focus and trust in the right direction. It will give entrance to the power, strength, and might of the Holy Spirit in your life. Bitterness, the direct opposite, places you in the arenas of strife, envy, revenge, confusion, illness, and double-mindedness. Bitterness creates a never-ending cycle that will eventually *take* your life. Forgiveness will *give* you life. Forgiveness keeps you in the Spirit and causes you to win every time. Don't fall into the trap of bitterness, my friend. See beyond the offenses, though they may be many, and soar in the Spirit. That's the first step to victory.

> **Forgiveness gives entrance to the power of the Holy Spirit in your life.**

PRIDE WILL CORRUPT

The next thing we must guard against to effectively go through an attack is *pride.* Sometimes when we have been hit with feeling worthless or rejected, we have a tendency to counteract by exalting ourselves. When we do this, we are in great danger.

How can the enemy trick us into pride when we think we are serving God?

I have seen minister after minister fall to this deception. They have been repeatedly hit by the attacks of the enemy in their doctrine, their stand for God, and in their personal lives. As a result, instead of staying pliable to the correcting voice of the Lord, they develop a shell of pride and enter into what I call the persecution complex. They think they are right no matter what comes their way. If you disagree with them, they think you have a devil. They think everyone is out to get them. Instead of hearing the voice of the Lord, they submit to a lifestyle of constant and *self-induced* persecution. They will even pervert Scripture to defend themselves. They go across the line and eventually think if you are not under constant attack, you are doing nothing for God.

A persecution complex will cause us to do flaky spiritual things. It causes us to go into isolation and think everyone and everything is a devil. We can get a hardness about us and think it is the strength and boldness of the Lord. That pride will take us into the next phase: the confrontation complex.

Confrontation is good, and it is godly. It has its place, and we cannot be afraid of it. It is a part of the gospel. But we abuse confrontation when we shove obnoxious boldness and exaggerated lifestyles on people. Confrontation must only come from the *unction* of the Spirit, not the *emotion* of a groomed personality. Only pride that has seasoned itself from hurts and wounds causes persecution and confrontation complexes. It deceives us into thinking we are winning and gaining ground, when in reality we are losing steadily the glory of God in our lives.

Many spiritual calls and destinies have been aborted by this area of pride. Instead of effectively going through the attack, this pride causes them to take a side road and fall prey to it.

It may be true that we are seasoned and mature. We may know many things according to the Word of God. But we must know it in the Spirit and feed what we know by the laws of the Spirit. To be effective, we must be strong in *all* areas of the Word, not just a portion of it. Specializing and emphasizing just a portion of the Word, feeding on those truths alone and refusing to humble ourselves to the whole counsel, will cause us to fall. We cannot point a finger at the world and pervert

> **We must be strong in all areas of the Word, not just a portion.**

a spiritual truth by thinking we are absolutely invincible. We cannot arrogantly attack everything that hits us and not hear the voice of the Lord first and foremost. *It may be our own correction that will cause us to win in the battle.*

You must examine your heart, your life, your trust, and your focus in order to win and stay accurate during an attack.

Kathryn Kuhlman was constantly attacked in her ministry by religious leaders, friends, and the media. She never reacted in pride. She never took on a persecution complex, although she had natural reason to do so. Even in the time she personally stumbled, she regained her strength in a way that should teach us all. Her ministry retained such a presence of God that even when she walked into the California studios, her presence could be felt. Despite the multitudes healed and saved in her services, no one left looking at Miss Kuhlman. God took her from glory to glory, worldwide, despite the persecution and attacks.

The basic principle remains the same. Miss Kuhlman said over and over in her ministry, "I know where I came from, and I know better than anyone else what makes this ministry what it is. It's certainly not Kathryn Kuhlman."

That's the way we have to be. We make ourselves available to be used of God, despite the attacks. It is not our ability nor our intellect that works the victory. *It is the working of the Holy Spirit through a clean vessel that accomplishes it.*

James wrote to give us another foundation to effectively win in the battle:

> *God resisteth the proud, but giveth grace unto the humble. Submit yourselves therefore to God. Resist the devil, and he will flee from you.* (James 4:6–7)

We must stay hooked into the Vine. (See John 15:1–11.) We must not think we are a special breed because we are anointed and called. Special breeds die early because they unhook from the Vine. They are deceived into thinking they have all the nutrients they need. They get out on their own with what little they know, and they fall. Stay grafted into the Vine. The Vine gives the boldness, strength, and victory we need to come forth in accuracy and progression.

> **Stay grafted into the Vine for the boldness, strength, and victory.**

Once we have realized that our true enemy is not in the natural and have rid ourselves of pride, then we can effectively go through a battle, use our weapons, and win.

WEAPON NUMBER ONE

The apostle Paul wrote in Ephesians 6:13,

Wherefore take unto you the whole armour of God, that ye may be able to withstand in the evil day, and having done all, to stand.

There are several words in that Scripture that denote action on our part. No matter how beat up and drained we feel, if we have understood the principles we just discussed, our hearts will be in position for action.

Acquaint yourself with the Word of God, your sword, in the areas of faith, truth, healing, deliverance, prosperity, salvation, joy, peace, and soundness. The only thing that wounds the enemy is the sword of the Spirit, or the Word of God. (See Ephesians 6:14-17.) The Word must be strong in you. It is your security. The anointing of God can help fix your problems, but the Word of God keeps that anointing fixed.

God called us soldiers, not weak-kneed babies.

Also, you must choose to believe the Word. Hebrews 10:35 says, *"Cast not away therefore your confidence, which hath great recompense of reward."*

The Word of God is your confidence. If you will cling to it and make it a part of you, the reward will be great. When it comes down to a brutal attack, then you must fight against it with brutal trust. The devil will try to tell you that God is not going to do anything for you and that you're not going to make it. Choose to believe God and His Word. You must make a conscious choice to keep your confidence and to not cast away what belongs to you. Don't wait for an emotional outburst. Don't wait for a personal prophecy or a minister to come through and lay hands on you. Don't wait for a visit from heaven. *Just choose to believe.* I know it is hard sometimes, but God didn't call us weak-kneed babies. He called us soldiers. Get in there and believe the Word!

You've got to be aggressive with the Word of God and allow it to work for you. Christians who keep waiting will never receive what is theirs. Ruthlessly believe the Word of God. Run out to meet it. Don't live by sovereign acts; live by faith.

What does it mean to live by faith during an attack? It means to *do*, to *walk*, to *journey*. Faith causes destiny to form and come to you. If all you can do at this point is read a verse and say, "God, I believe that," then do it. That is aggressive faith. Sometimes just a "string" of belief will keep you going. Don't feel guilty about that. God accepts you and will come to your aid if you will believe. It doesn't matter if the devil has come and stolen almost everything you have, you still have something left. If you are doing all that you can, then keep doing it! New strength will come, and you will win.

God will come to your aid if you will believe.

Holding to the Word is not complicated; it is the will to dig into it that is hard under an attack. Just remember, no matter what it looks like in the natural, if you will hold to that thread of belief until more strength comes, you'll make it. Faith is not three thousand confessions. Sometimes there's just enough time to say, "I believe" and swing on that cord.

Do not let the enemy speak lies to your mind. Fire back at him with the accurate Scriptures you know. We shut the mouths of lions with the Word of God. Instead of a roar, you'll hear a whimpering retreat. The devil is afraid of the strength in the Spirit. So scare him! When more strength comes to you, then learn to use more of the Word.

When you unite yourself with the Word of God, He can effectively use the rest of His weapons of war through you.

WEAPON NUMBER TWO

With the Word of God in me, these next Scriptures are the ones I use to survive a spiritual war. These Scriptures will keep us strong in God if we do what they say.

Paul said,

And be not drunk with wine, wherein is excess; but be filled with the Spirit; speaking to yourselves in psalms and hymns and spiritual songs, singing and making melody in your heart to the Lord. (Ephesians 5:18–19)

Paul encouraged us to stay filled with the Spirit. If we stay filled with God, it will keep us in strength and joy despite what is going on around us. How do we stay filled? He told us: speaking to ourselves in psalms, hymns, and spiritual songs. Then we sing and make melody to ourselves and to Him.

If we go back into the book of Psalms, we find every situation that David went through, and how God delivered him from them all and showed Himself strong. David sang most of these to himself or to the Lord, and they caused him to be lifted and strengthened. The Psalms are explicit in describing the way we can feel about certain situations without condemnation. It's called being real with God. Every time we are real with God and cry out to Him, He shows His strength to us.

David would say, "Lord, the devils, these enemies, are all about me, ready to consume my flesh." Or, "God, this friend I trusted in wants to take my life." Or, "Break the bones of your enemies, O God." Then he would sing, "Bless the Lord, O my soul, for You are very great." Or, "I will sing of mercy and judgment, unto You, Lord, will I sing." Or, "As the hart pants for water, so my soul longs for You, O God."

He was singing those words from his heart as a melody. The spirit man (the spirit that we have inside) makes those words, and as they flow out of you, give them to God. When you do that, you will begin to make songs that will encourage your own heart and help you out.

The Psalms, just like the rest of the Word, have a continual anointing upon them. I've written several down that have ministered to me. Sometimes I put my own melody to them from my spirit. They are in me so deeply, they come out when I least expect it. I'll be through with a meeting, standing there looking at everyone, and all of a sudden this song that had been in my heart will burst out.

Often a staff member will look at me and say, "Where did that come from?" I have learned to say, "It's good! Let it go." Those songs come from your spirit to give you life and encouragement. Through your spirit, the Holy Spirit will witness and speak to you. Many times, when you are singing to God, He will begin to sing right out of you and give you an answer.

Many times when you sing to God, He will sing out of you and speak to you.

I can remember when I was in my worst war, those songs would start way down deep in me. They would be just a small little voice. I kept giving place to it, and by the end of the day, I would come out real bold. I would sit on my bed and sing. Sometimes, even when I would ache inside, the songs of the Spirit would still come. I would sing for hours. I would say over and over, "God, I believe in You." It didn't matter what was happening around me. Sometimes I would write the things that were inside of me out on paper. That's what David and others did in Psalms. They wrote the melodies inside of them for others to see and receive life. That's what hymns are: written melodies from hearts crying out and rejoicing to God, proclaiming Him as Lord despite the battles.

Don't be afraid to pour your heart out to God. Cleansing comes when you do that. The devil tells you, "If you say what you really feel, that is doubt." God understands you and knows how you feel anyway. Sometimes you have to have that release to get the garbage out of you. You have to say, "God, here it comes, but I still believe." Remember that, and let it go.

Sometimes you can get so caught up in the mechanics of faith you forget the character of God. In all of your journeys, in all of your battles, in all of your situations, always remember that, when you come to Jesus, He receives. He doesn't cast you out. No matter where you are, no matter what you look like, if you come believing, you are accepted. The mercy and strength of God will restore you back to where you belong.

> **Let the words of the Psalms carry you into the blessedness of the Spirit.**

When you make melody from your heart, life will come from heaven and keep you going. If you don't have life, you don't win. God will move for you, but sometimes you have to prime the pump. Do you know what I mean by that? Go over into the book of Psalms, and let those anointed words carry you out into the blessedness of the Spirit. Then, just catch up to it and sing your own songs.

You may say, "Well, I just don't know if that is necessary."

If Paul encouraged you to do it, if Moses and Miriam did it as they saw the victory, and if David did it when he was in the midst of war, then those are just three big examples you need to learn from and practice today. When your church is in a war, when you are under attack and feel you are getting weak, then one thing you need to do is let the songs of the Spirit come out of your mouth. Let them soar and sing them loud. Don't be embarrassed. Your own ears need to hear it!

Make your head take account. Make your head line up and listen to what your spirit is saying. Your whole war may just be in your head, and the words of the Spirit will soothe the mental part of man. Words can soothe or disturb. The songs of the Spirit will cause peace to come into a disturbed mind, a disturbed flesh, and a disturbed heart. Songs of the Spirit cause peace in the midst of a great storm. They will give you the strength to continue and win in the battle. These melodies will bring your soul back to common sense so it can be renewed. They restore your position in the spirit.

Praise and worship is a traveling vehicle. It causes you to travel into the good things of the Lord. It causes you to have an understanding of the greatness, the almightiness, and the awesomeness of God. When we sing and worship from our hearts, He comes down. (See John 4:23–24.) Praise and worship create a balance for you during attack. Many times, during a battle, it seems as if God is nowhere. These kinds of songs will give you a God-consciousness and keep you from being totally devil-conscious. In other words, as much as you are under attack, you must worship to stay accurate.

You don't have to wait to go to church where there are musical instruments. You don't have to have a music leader. You do exactly what the Scripture says. You make music in your heart, by yourself. It may sound dead and dry. If that discourages you, then go back to the book of Psalms and read some more. Stay there and let it put your heart in position. Pretty soon, you will begin to get encouraged, and songs will come out of you. You'll sing about your situation, about all the problems, and many times the Lord will sing out the answer.

The songs of the Lord work as a weapon. They stop the condemnation and onslaught of the enemy in your life.

Many years ago, I took my first trip to Africa. I was in the nation of Mozambique, and it was a Communist country. They were at war and didn't like Americans too well, but I felt led of the Lord to go, so I obeyed and went.

I had felt in my spirit that there was going to be some type of military action, and it came to me so strongly that I knew it would happen. I had thought that it would be on the way into the country. As I entered in from Zimbabwe, I saw

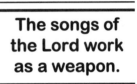

The songs of the Lord work as a weapon.

all kinds of buildings that had been blown up. I just sat there and continued to pray protection Scriptures over myself.

There was no mishap, and I preached in a little grass hut Assembly of God church that night. As a matter of fact, I slept in the church when the service was over. The next day everything was going in a normal manner. I thought, *Well, maybe my meditation and praying stopped everything. Maybe I was supposed to pray and prevent,* so I forgot about it and climbed in the back of an old truck taking me back to Zimbabwe.

As I began to sleep in the back of that truck, gunfire woke me up. Someone yelled, "Get out of the truck!" Well, being as young as I was at the time, I stood up and looked around. Not being used to that kind of situation, I thought the bullets flying over my head had to be meant for someone else—not me!

By the grace of God, I finally realized those bullets were meant for my body and my life and I had better take some natural covering. So I got in a ditch and laid down and prayed. A good part of this story is that I was not afraid. Up to that time, John Wayne movies were about the extent of my military awareness! I didn't really know what was going on and how dangerous it actually was. I remember telling my angels that if I died, they were getting it on the way up!

When the encounter ended, several people had been shot, and some died. We got back in the truck, and then I got scared. As I started again on the way to Zimbabwe, I just began to worship and pray to ease myself. I kept saying to the Lord, "I thought a good man's steps were ordered by the Lord. Did I miss it?"

As I sat there and kept plugging heaven for an answer, it suddenly came back to me. I remember it as clear as yesterday. It seemed as if a little breeze came to me, and I began to sing for half an hour or more. I sang in tongues for a while. There are times when you can sing in tongues by choice and times you can sing in your natural language by choice. But there are also times that the Spirit will unction you, and it comes out of you in both tongues and natural language. You can tell the difference. It has more force to it when it comes by the Spirit. It "booms" out of you. (See 1 Corinthians 14:4.)

When the gifts of the Spirit come to you this way, you don't have to have someone to interpret. You can interpret yourself. That's what happened to me that day. As I began to sing, the Lord began to speak right out of me. He began to speak the answer and the causes back to me. He told me of His protection and His reasons. See, that song came right up out of me and satisfied my soul, my flesh, and my spirit. I was at peace with what happened that day, and it never bothered me again.

When melodies come from your heart, they will come in a perfect flow, rhythm and all. Sometimes you'll say words you didn't even know how to say before. It's fun to hear how the Spirit orchestrates and causes the words to rhyme. Do you know why it's fun? Because it produces life.

> **When melodies come from your heart, it produces life.**

Begin to enter into the songs from your heart. They will put you in remembrance of how great God is. As you sing these kinds of songs, God will be bigger to you than any problem you face. These songs will produce great joy and, as a result, great strength.

WEAPON NUMBER THREE

Once you have opened your heart to God, it will be easy to do what James 5:16 says:

Confess your faults one to another, and pray one for another, that ye may be healed. The effectual fervent prayer of a righteous man availeth much.

Another way to say that verse is, "Once you have forgiven one another, then the unceasing prayer that is united spirit, soul, and body will prevail over circumstances and be of much strength."

Sometimes we focus so keenly on the latter part of that verse, we forget the first part of it.

If your attack has come through another person, you must forgive the person and their actions. No matter how hard it seems now, begin to speak forgiveness out of your mouth. If you are strong in your purpose and intent, your heart will soon follow the words you speak. According to this verse, it is only *after* we forgive that our prayers can be effectual and fervent, availing much. How can a prayer be heard by God and produce great results if it is prayed from a heart filled with bitterness and revenge? If you have purposely filled yourself with the Spirit of God (Weapon #2), then there is no room for offense and bitterness.

It doesn't matter how feeble you feel or how weak your words start out. Remember, Jesus will never turn you away; He hears your *heart* over your words. God is not complicated. When you're under attack, any prayer you offer to God (supported spirit, soul, and body) will produce results if your heart desires His will. Sometimes we think we have to groan and travail for hours to get a result. If you have the strength to do that under attack and are led by His Spirit, by all means do it.

No matter how feeble your words, Jesus will listen and hear your heart.

But we have to be careful to keep religion out of our definition of prayer. Prayer is simply talking to God. It is not a formula or a ritual. I like what my grandmother says when people come to her and say they can't pray. She answers, "Well, you can talk to your father, can't you? Talk to God the same way." When I was under my heaviest attack, I knew that even my thoughts toward God counted as a prayer to Him.

Fervent prayer produces results. What do I mean by fervent? We have three parts to our being: spirit, soul, and body. Jesus said in Matthew 12:25,

Every kingdom divided against itself is brought to desolation; and every city or house divided against itself shall not stand.

As individuals, we are a "kingdom" consisting of a spirit, soul, and body. Therefore, you are not a mind. You are a *spirit* that owns a *mind* that lives in a *body*.

If these three parts of your kingdom are divided, you'll fall. If your mind is planning your next business venture, party, or vacation; your body wants to go to sleep; and your spirit is not leading them, you're divided. That is not a prayer that is fervent. It will not see results.

Prayer during an attack starts from the same source as any other spiritual arena: It comes by choice. It takes willpower to grab hold of all three parts and make yourself go into prayer concerning your situation. During a spiritual attack, chaos hits. Everything, both inside and outside of you, is out of order. It takes an active decision on your part to pull yourself back in line.

A person who has not made that decision will face three different directions. He won't know which way to go or what to believe. He can go the body way and try to forget his problems through the flesh, or he can go the mind way and live in paranoia and confusion. Or he can choose the spirit's way and pull everything back in the proper arena.

Spiritual attacks will paralyze you. They try to frighten you by worry and fear, frustrating you into doing nothing. As a result, your body will not obey you, your mind will talk you out of or into whatever comes its way, and you'll fall. A kingdom divided cannot stand. The devil defeats you by dividing you.

Also, fervent does not mean "scared faith." Scared faith is a little bit of fear mixed with a little faith. God didn't say that scared faith works; He said fervent prayer works. In an attack, it doesn't matter how small your faith may seem; just stay fervent in it. Don't be overwhelmed by the entire situation around you; just stick to one thing at a time.

The mind cannot properly focus on a variety of things at one time. Fervent prayer is focused. It is prayer that believes. Start with the most important thing to you, and fervently pray and believe God for the answer and the help. It doesn't matter if all the details of the situation are intertwined. Start with the most important detail and stick to that one. The answer will come because you will have the faith to believe for it. As soon as the peace comes, then move on to deal with the next situation.

> **It doesn't matter how small your faith may seem; just stay fervent in it.**

When you pray under an attack, don't be frustrated if it feels like your prayer only hits the ceiling. Just have enough faith to believe God reached down and got it. If we feel condemned by thinking our prayers didn't go anywhere, it will make us quit. Remember that any amount of faith goes a long way, even if you do not feel at your highest or best.

When you are under a heavy spiritual attack, you are limited by your natural language. God has made a help for us in times of trouble; He is the Holy Spirit.

Likewise the Spirit also helpeth our infirmities [weaknesses]: for we know not what we should pray for as we ought: but the Spirit itself maketh intercession for us with groanings which cannot be uttered. And he that searcheth the hearts knoweth what is the mind of the Spirit, because he maketh intercession for the saints according to the will of God.   (Romans 8:26–27)

Some have misinterpreted this Scripture as referring to our own human spirit or our own mind. Our own mind is limited and cannot always speak what is accurate. This text is referring to God's Holy Spirit who dwells inside the believer. The Holy Spirit is always there to lead us into the correct answer.

The Bible tells us that He will come to our aid, energize us, and pray through us to the perfect will of God in the situation. Strong, spiritual tongues have a place in the believer's life. The Scripture says that, when we have said everything we know to say from our natural minds, the Spirit Himself will pray the highest form of prayer through us by words that cannot be articulated. The Spirit of God knows the will of God in every situation. When we allow Him to pray through us, the correct answer comes to our spirit, and our minds can interpret it and know what to do.

Groanings of the spirit can only come by the Spirit's unction, *not* from a preplanned emotion. The Bible speaks in Exodus of God answering and delivering the people as He heard their groanings. But these *human* groanings of grief and despair were only *symbolic* of the manifestation of the Spirit of God in the book of Romans. We must be careful not to get into works of the flesh when we deal with a spiritual situation. The Spirit of God is ready and willing to link up with you and pray the perfect will of God in every situation.

Believe that our angels will work on our behalf. Hebrews 1:14 speaks of our angels and says, *"Are they not all ministering* [serving] *spirits, sent forth to minister for them who shall be heirs of salvation?"*

In Matthew 4:11, when the attack against Jesus was over, the Bible says the angels came and ministered to Him. Because we are heirs through Jesus Christ, God assigns angels to us. We must use every weapon God has provided for us to win the battle, in Jesus' name. The cleansing of our hearts, the Word of God, and the knowledge and understanding of what strong prayer can do will lead us into total victory every time.

CHAPTER

FOUR

THE SOUL UNDER ATTACK

There is one great rule we must always remember: *Wounds left unattended attract evil spirits.*

In the natural, whenever an animal is badly wounded, vultures follow it and circle it. When the animal is down, they attack and eat their prey. These dumb and skimpy birds do nothing to cause the downfall of their prey; they just take advantage of it and help it die. The same is true in the spirit realm.

When a hurt or wound is left unattended, in any area of our lives, it attracts the enemy. He will follow you, circle you, and aggravate you until that hurt causes your downfall. If it is not dealt with, he will feed upon it until you are consumed. Many have left the ministry, left their mates, or left their destinies because they did not recover from a hurt.

We cannot play with hurts and wounds. We can't pretend they will go away if we don't think about them. Hurts and wounds that have not been tended are the primary cause of pain in believers who need deliverance. Although believers *cannot* be possessed in their spirits, they can go through similar stages in their souls and bodies. Those stages are *oppression, depression,* and *obsession.*

Satan wars against the soul of man. The main problem of this decade will not be fear of war, the AIDS epidemic, or homelessness. The number one problem of this decade will be mental illness. A great struggle for the soul of man will take place. Even as we look around the world today, we observe a war on the minds of people.

Even the media has discerned this problem. Commercials used to feature toothpaste and orange juice. Now we see ads for help with abuse and mental problems. There is one ad that shows a nice-looking young man lying on his bed at home. His parents walk in and yell at him, "Why can't you work? Why can't you get up and go to school? What's your problem? You are so lazy!" Then the announcer comes on and says, "He's not physically ill. He is mentally ill. If you are like this or know someone who is, call this toll-free number." What's happening to our world? We're in a struggle over the soul of man.

TWO DEVICES

According to Scripture, two devices are used to thwart the soul of man. First Peter 2:11 says, *"Dearly beloved, I beseech you as strangers and pilgrims, abstain from fleshly lusts, which war against the soul."*

One problem that wars against the soul of man is the lust of the flesh. The natural arena, or lust of the flesh, is bountiful in the world today. I call it the natural arena because these attacks come by things we can explicitly see with our natural eyes. Many have paid a serious price in their souls for being deeply involved with it. The good news is that no problem is too big or too ugly for God to heal and make right.

The second problem that wars against the soul of man takes place in the spiritual arena. It takes the Word and the maturing of our inner man to fight these attacks, because in the spiritual arena, we cannot see with our natural eyes. The consequences of these attacks remain unseen unless we are alerted by our inner man. This area, where the devil wages his main attack, will be the focus of our discussion.

The spiritual arena has often been camouflaged and ignored. This is mainly due to our ignorance on how to effectively overcome the problems we don't understand. In Matthew 22:37, Jesus admonished a Pharisee by saying, *"Thou shalt love the Lord thy God with all thy heart, and with all thy soul, and with all thy mind."*

> **Maintaining a clear and free soul opens the door for the love of God in us.**

This exhortation clearly shows the arenas the enemy attacks. If our enemy can keep our souls preoccupied and tormented, then we are unable to fulfill the plan of God for our lives. Maintaining clear and free souls opens the door for the love of God in us. As a result, He can fulfill His purpose through us.

Third John 2 states, *"Beloved, I wish above all things that thou mayest prosper and be in health, even as thy soul prospereth."*

It is true that our spirit is perfect, complete, and mature through Jesus Christ. But the prospering of our soul determines the effect we have on the earth.

ARENAS OF THE HUMAN SOUL

Many in the church have often misunderstood the soul of man; usually they ignore it. The believer experiences an element of fear when it comes to understanding the soul. God created every part of the soul of man, and we must replace the fear of it with the truth of the Word in order to understand ourselves. God meant for every part of our being to be used to its greatest potential.

There are five key areas to the human soul: *The will, the emotions, the intellect, the imagination, and the memory.*

God created all five of these areas and designed them to be maintained and used according to His Word. Each area of your soul is to be generated by your spirit. The Holy Spirit, through your spirit man, should inspire and influence your will, your emotions, your intellect, your imagination, and your memory.

Unless we understand how the enemy attacks our souls, the desire of the Spirit will not manifest through us. When we have unharnessed souls, their desires will be the dominating factor in our lives. Although our spirits are secure the minute we are born again, our souls are being constantly renewed. In the Philippians 2:12, Paul exhorted us to work out our own salvation. In other words, we are to constantly renew our souls with the Word of God and stand against attacks.

God meant for every part of our being to be used to its greatest potential.

When an attack hits, the spirit man always bounces back faster than the soul. The soul must learn to regroup and strengthen itself through the Word of God. Sitting under strong, anointed preaching helps to line up your soul. Accurate praise and worship also enables the soul to pursue God and win.

We have the ability to understand our will, emotions, intellect, imagination, memory, and to walk by maturity through each one. We can possess our whole man. If we are fighting a battle in our souls, we must purpose in our hearts to win in it. Neutrality in any form spells defeat. We must move forward *internally* before an outward manifestation is seen. *An internal security will always produce an outward stability.*

In the following chapters, we will discuss the five areas of the soul, as well as the spiritual attacks against each one.

CHAPTER

5

FIVE

THE WILL UNDER ATTACK

The will is the dominant force of the human soul. It doesn't matter if you are born again or not, *the human will has the final say in any decision.*

God created humankind with a will. He doesn't want robots to love and serve Him. He receives pleasure from the choice we make with our will to serve Him. Our praise and worship delight Him because they come from a choice to do it. We decide if we go to heaven or hell. God didn't make the lake of fire for us. It was made for the devil and his angels; but we can go live and burn there forever if we choose. God made heaven for those who love Him and want to live with Him. It's that simple.

We choose whether we will serve God or the devil. We decide whether we will give in to sin or live in purity. Even after we are born again, we decide if we experience the things of God or just go to church on Sunday. Even when the call to ministry comes, we still decide to accept it or reject it.

The human will is sovereign. God will not violate it. We cannot make wrong decisions and then blame God for the outcome. Responsibility comes with the human will. Those who refuse to be responsible and choose to live however they please prefer to blame God for their trouble and calamity. But He is not responsible for our choices—*we are.*

FUNCTION OF THE WILL

How can you know the working of the human will over the rest of the soul? Let me give you an example everyone can relate to. Let's say that you've just finished a huge meal and dessert is being brought to the table. Your mother has just made your favorite chocolate cake, but you know you shouldn't eat another bite.

Suddenly, your *imagination* comes in and you think, *I just know that creamy fudge icing is heaped on that cake.* Your *memory* moves in, "Remember how rich and moist that cake is? Remember how great it tasted last Christmas?" The *emotions* chide, "You know how much fun it was eating

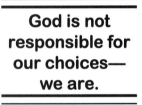

God is not responsible for our choices— we are.

Mom's chocolate cake." Your *mind* begins to signal the rest of the body, your *eyes* focus on the cake, your *mouth* begins to water, your *stomach* is full but says, "I'll make room!" and out of nowhere *the will steps* in and shouts, "NO!"

That ends it right there. The rest of your soul and body rebels, but your will made a decision and that's the final word. Every other part of you has to line up to whatever the will says.

That's a fun illustration, but it helps us to identify the other parts of the soul and helps us to see the importance of the will. The same is true in the spirit realm. When the rest of your soul wants to get out of line, the will has the authority to bring you back on track. That's why it doesn't matter how we feel in order to gain a result. We will always feel either up or down, but the will is our mainstay. Our will always makes the final decision, wrong or right. Our will is the strongest part of our soulish being.

When the will obeys the Word and the Spirit of God, the rest of the soul soon follows. Our emotions are forced to feel the right way, and our minds are trained to think on the right things. The human will is the disciplinary factor of the soul.

The human will is not automatically born again when the spirit is. The Word and the unction within us must transform our will to serve God and fulfill His purpose on earth. The human will begins to function before birth. Even as a fetus inside the mother, the baby uses the will to move its arms and legs. Once it is born, the parents have the job of training the will of the child. When a child has a temper tantrum or similar outbursts, it does not come from the emotions or the intellect. It comes from an uncontrolled will that must learn discipline and control.

When we are born again, our wills begin to change. The rebellion in our hearts toward God can't come as easily. We now have wills to serve Him. We now have wills to do what is right and pleasing to Him. From the moment of new birth, our wills are to be submitted to the plan of God and ceased to be our own. From that day forward, God intended for our wills to be *disciplined and trained by His Word*. A will seasoned by the Word will produce life, health, and joy. It will always cause us to make choices that produce increase and abundance. The circumstances surrounding us will be irrelevant.

No greater joy exists than to merge the human will into the will of God. The greatest experience on earth is knowing we have linked our wills with the will of the Father. In doing so, all of heaven supports our every effort. The greatest strength on earth comes from knowing God is pleased and walks beside us. When the human will and the will of God become as one, we are invincible. No foe can stand; no attack can conquer; no disease can destroy; and no curse can come.

> **No greater joy exists than to merge the human will with the will of God.**

The problem comes when we don't know or understand the power of our human will. However, our enemy understands our potential. He knows his defeat is sure, unless he can sway our will.

THE WILL OF THE ENEMY

Just as we have a will, Satan himself has a will. God created him as a beautiful archangel, a chief musician in heaven who led worship to the Father. But through his will, he followed the lust of pride and thought *he* would take over the throne of God. (See Isaiah 14:12–14.) As a result, he was kicked out of heaven like lightning. (See Luke 10:18.) *By his will,* he changed his status from Lucifer to Satan. God didn't create Satan; He made Lucifer. But, through a choice of his will, Lucifer perverted his own destiny. By his choice, he forever curses himself. He is now Satan, the enemy of God and humanity. His demons have a will also. They willfully carry out the plans of their leader and vow to faithfully fulfill them.

In the book of John we can read a very familiar verse that explains the will of the enemy: *"The thief comes only in order to steal and kill and destroy"* (John 10:10 AMP).

The goal of the enemy is to steal your will for God. In doing so, he can eventually destroy you. When your will for God crumbles, poverty, sickness, disease, calamity, and disaster come. He robs your joy and strength from you through your lack of willpower. Passive decisions or a lack of will can even cause physical death.

DEMONIC RESULTS

How does the human will go under the attack of the enemy? Through passivity and lethargy. Passivity and lethargy are the major killers of spiritual life. *Merriam-Webster's 11th Collegiate Dictionary* defines these words as, "lacking energy or will" and "abnormal drowsiness," respectively.

We are to be an excited, courageous, creative, and enthusiastic people. When we say yes to God, a whole new world opens up and places us on the cutting edge. New joy, life, and strength come to us.

When we say yes to God, new joy, life, and strength come to us.

When the human will is under attack, we may lose our zeal for God. Suddenly, we couldn't care less if the gospel is ever preached again. We become lazy, careless, and slothful. Our discipline and diligence evaporate. Indecisiveness becomes the predominant factor in our lives. We can't see or hear what is wrong or right. Instead of the godly strength to produce and live by our decisions, we rely on the opinions of others. What another man *says* carries more weight than what we *know* in our hearts. If we are not careful, we end up confused and doubting, tossed about by everything we hear.

How can the enemy cause a human will to become passive? *Through constant vexation or harassment.* We must understand that the enemy very rarely hits one time. Instead, he constantly, day in and day out, beats against what we stand for until we are worn out. When he has beat our will to a thread, and we have not renewed ourselves by the Word of God, then one major hit will knock us out. That's why we wake up one morning and find ourselves in sin. That's why we look around one day and find marriages in shambles. That's why some marry the wrong person. It's because their wills were made weak through constant vexation.

THE WILL OF SAMSON

Let's look at a biblical example of a strong will made weak by the enemy.

In the thirteenth chapter of the book of Judges, a man named Samson was born of great physical strength. This man had a great destiny. Before his birth, an angel appeared to his mother and said that her son would begin to deliver the Israelites from the enemy. This angel also told her the conditions of his strength and what he must do in order to perform the will of God for his people.

Samson had a wonderful childhood. Scripture tells us that the Spirit of the Lord came upon him many times during his youth. He tore a lion apart with his bare hands and slew a thousand men with the jawbone of a donkey.

But Samson had one problem: He loved the women of the world and chose them over the women of God. Because Samson did not follow the Word of God for his life, he opened the door for the enemy to destroy him. Samson's strength was directly linked to his will. Had his will been submitted to God, he would have been invincible. He would have had not only physical strength but also the spiritual strength to say "No!"

when the enemy came. But through repeated sinful pleasures, his human will was weakened by a stronger human will: the will of Delilah.

The Philistines were the enemies of the people of God. They had kept the people of God in bondage for years. The only wall between them and the Israelites was the strength of their leader, Samson. The Philistines reasoned that they could only capture Samson through the woman he loved. No physical strength could capture him. No army had been able to contain him. So they approached Delilah and offered her a bribe. Her job was to make Samson tell her the secret of his strength. Because she came from the camp of the enemy and her love for money exceeded her love for Samson, she obliged.

Three different times she whined and begged Samson to tell her his secret. Although he tricked her those three times, his will became weaker and weaker. Finally, the fourth time came:

> *And she said unto him, How canst thou say, I love thee, when thine heart is not with me? thou hast mocked me these three times, and hast not told me wherein thy great strength lieth. And it came to pass, when she pressed him daily with her words, and urged him, so that his soul was vexed unto death; that he told her all his heart.* (Judges 16:15–17)

Samson's will was pressed and vexed until he succumbed. As a result, he was robbed of his strength and taken into captivity. In the end, as he cried out for the mercy of God, more Philistines were killed than ever before, but Samson died with them.

As believers, we must fight for and protect our wills for God. As we deeply plant the Word of God into our wills, the plan of God becomes easier to follow. With the Word as our substance, we find it easier to stand against the schemes of the enemy. When controversy comes, we will have the strength to shout "No!" in the face of trouble.

That kind of strength is discussed in Ephesians 6:13. It says,

Wherefore take unto you the whole armour of God, that ye may be able to withstand in the evil day, and having done all, to stand.

Although our own strength alone accomplishes nothing, our will fused into the will of God enables us to stand through any attack the enemy brings. Our human will can only be strengthened through the Word of God. When God's will is joined with our will, we will not wear out under pressure. Godly strength produces endurance and patience.

Inward security produces outward stablility.

Outwardly, our physical strength can only stand for so long. We can perform certain feats for God in our own physical strength, but they will not last. Remember that inward security produces outward stability. When the inner man is strong, the will latches on to it. As a result, the works we do for God will be lasting and have great effect in the earth.

I've seen many strong men and women fall into the trap of relying on their own strength for the ministry. They get so caught up in the works of God, they fail to renew themselves and keep their inner man strong. It comes to a point where they cannot discern between their own physical strength and the strength of God through them. Sadly, the works they accomplish fall away and become a spectacle to believers and sinners alike. *Our physical strength, or human will, cannot fight spiritual battles without the strength of God.*

I must also point out that we must not confuse the gifts of God, or the anointing, with the strength of God. Just because you have an anointing from God to heal the sick does not mean your will is linked with God's will. Do not confuse the two, because the gifts from God are another subject entirely. We have a responsibility to build up our inner man through the Word of God, *in spite of our accomplishments,* great or small.

I've told this story before, but it is worth telling again. In my grandparents' day, there was a minister greatly used in the gifts of God. He had such a power-ful anointing that all he had to do was raise his hand, and everyone in the prayer line would be slain in the spirit at once. Many healings took place. Yet he ran off with one of the women in the church and divorced his wife. It really bothered me that something like that could happen.

The whole armor of God must be grafted into your will.

What was the problem? He had a weak will. He had not taken the time to build his inner man and make it strong. When the attack of the enemy came, he fell and caused countless others to slander the gospel. *He relied on his gift as his strength.* The gifts are extra my friend. Where the rubber meets the road is in whether or not your human will merges with the will of God in every situation. The whole armor of God, or the principles of the Word of God, *must* be grafted into your will.

In this decade, God is requiring more from us as lead-ers and believers. Maturity and discernment must come forth from the body of Christ. God will require an answer for our accomplishments, whether they were lasting and accurate or weak and failing. Our goal should be a lasting accomplishment, not a spiritual explosion for the moment.

Samson, through his weakened will, fell during an attack of the enemy. His accomplishments were short lived. I've said in many of my meetings that, had Samson developed a stronger inner man and learned by his will to say "no," the book of Judges would have been longer. He would have accomplished more for the kingdom of God, and there would have been more to write about. Instead, we can learn a sad but important message from his life.

THE WILL OF JOSEPH

A man named Joseph can also teach us a great lesson. Although Joseph made minor mistakes in the beginning of his call, he learned from them and turned them into godly strength. He faced a similar situation, but the inner strength he had developed caused his will to remain strong and fixed with God's will.

In Genesis 39, we begin reading the portion I want to illustrate. Joseph had been sold in slavery to an Egyptian officer named Potiphar. Because Joseph's inner man was strong, God prospered him and caused great favor to be upon him. Potiphar trusted him and promoted him as overseer of his entire household.

This is where the enemy likes to operate. *Many times, he will wait until great favor and recognition come to us before he launches his greatest attack.* If we have not prepared our inner man, we can be caught up in the glory and workings of it all and fall into his schemes. This is where many strong leaders have fallen.

We can begin reading of the attack in verse seven:

And it came to pass after these things, that his master's wife cast her eyes upon Joseph; and she said, Lie with me. But he refused, and said unto his master's wife, Behold, my master wotteth not what is with me in the house, and he hath committed all that he hath to my hand; there is none greater in this house than I; neither hath he kept back any thing from me but thee, because thou art his wife: how then can I do this great wickedness, and sin against God? (Genesis 39:7–9)

Notice that Joseph's will strongly resisted this wrong. But one initial response doesn't shake the enemy. He continued his attack against Joseph, hoping to weaken his human will and cause him to fall. The enemy continued to harass and torment Joseph through this woman, hoping to wear out his will.

And it came to pass, as she spake to Joseph day by day, that he hearkened not unto her, to lie by her, or to be with her.

(verse 10)

Had Joseph's will not been fused with the will of God, this vexation would have caused him to fall. But Joseph was strong with the Word of God, and in the next verses we will see what he did to prove it:

And it came to pass about this time, that Joseph went into the house to do his business; and there was none of the men of the house there within. And she caught him by his garment, saying, Lie with me: and he left his garment in her hand, and fled, and got him out. (verses 11–12)

Joseph showed his inner strength by running away from the trouble. He was not cowardly in his action; he showed the enemy who was in control.

Years ago, the Spirit of God showed me that part of learning to run the race was knowing when to run away and when to stay. There is a time to run, just as there are times to stay and confront. Running the race of God is a spiritual art. In the New Testament, the apostle Paul sometimes confronted, and sometimes he fled.

In this particular instance, Joseph, in order to continue running the race, knew to run away so he could fulfill his destiny in purity. The unction of his spirit led him. Because his human will was immersed in the will of God, he knew exactly what to do.

> **Running the race of God is a spiritual art.**

Although the enemy falsely accused Joseph through Potiphar's wife (see Genesis 39:13–20), the accusation could not stand forever. The enemy plagued Joseph the best he could, but God always wins through us when our wills are submitted to Him. (See verse 21.) In the end, Pharaoh exalted Joseph and made him the second most powerful man in Egypt. Joseph was able to forgive the brothers who sold him into slavery, nations were saved from famine, and God was exalted.

Had Joseph succumbed, the attack of the enemy would have thwarted his destiny. Our enemy works the same today.

DEMONIC ATTACK

Spiritual attacks target the control of our will. If our will is broken, we will fall. By making sin attractive, the enemy aims to weaken our human will and cause us to fail God and humanity.

Understand that the devil cannot violate your will. He does not have the power to override it. He must have your permission to take you over. Even a nonbeliever has the willpower to say no to the devil. The Holy Spirit also will never override your human will. Instead, He speaks to it, witnesses to it, instructs it, but He will never violate it. The choice is your own.

The devil, on the other hand, wants to violate and control your will. He will wear it down by lies, tragedies, harassments, and bombardments until he owns it. If you easily yield your will over to his methods by falling prey to the circumstances he puts around you, your will weakens little by little. Before you know it, you have no strength left to fight, and he will own your will. You will suddenly find yourself giving in to everything he suggests or puts before you.

If you are being pressed daily, harassed, and tormented to fall into sin, then you are under a spiritual attack. The battle is over the control of your will. In order to win, you must begin to strengthen yourself through the Word of God. Find the Scriptures that deal with the trouble you are facing. Let strength and encouragement from the Word give you the courage to stand. Look the situation squarely in the face, and speak the Word of God to it. The Word of God is designed to handle the pressure. Adverse circumstances melt at the spoken Word. No matter how weak your will seems today, you are the one in control to make it stronger. Submit it to the will of God through the Word of God. *Receive what you read as a way of life.*

Let your will cause you to arise. By your will, receive the Word of God and let it walk you into nations. You can fulfill the call and destiny planned for you from the positive response of your will. Remember that eternal consequences are far greater than the temporary trials you face. The action of your will is eternal. Fight for what God has given you, and do not bow to the temporal onslaught against you. *The moment of trouble will pass; but the decisions you make will stand forever.*

CHAPTER

6

SIX

THE EMOTIONS
UNDER ATTACK

Just as God has given us a will, He has also given us emotions. The emotional side of humankind is a world all its own. In the past, due to lack of knowledge, emotions led the church at large. In reaction to this error, the church swayed to the other extreme, many came to believe it is unscriptural to feel anything. When they did, they learned to lie about it and say they hadn't. This teaching is as much in error as the previous.

The fact is, we do feel things in our soul, good or bad. It is not wrong to have emotions; *but it is wrong to have them out of control.* Our emotions create imbalance when we base the decisions of our lives around them.

God desires for us to have emotions. He gave them to us. But we are not to use them to manipulate or control another person. We are not to use them to find the will of God for our lives. We are not to use them to prove the Spirit of God is working in our lives. Our emotions are not the basis of true love, or the lack of it.

Just as color adds life to a black and white television show, so God created our emotions to do so in our individual lives. He did not make our emotions to rule us, but to enhance us. He made them to show detail and depth. He gave them to us to show His personality and character in the earth. God did not create them to be the sole expression of our being, neither did He create them to remain dormant.

> **God gave us emotions to show His personality and character.**

Just as the rest of our soul, the emotions must be matured through the Word of God. When we feel something contrary to the will of God, it is wrong. If we don't stop it there, our emotions will literally lead our lives by wrong desires. *Wrong emotions have the potential to steal your destiny for God.*

The emotional side of man, by nature, is unruly. It is an unharnessed frontier that the inner man must conquer. Our emotions must be steered and guided. When emotions manifest, they must have purpose behind them. When our inner man guides our emotions, great results are produced. When our spirits lead our emotions, it opens the door to manifest the mercy of God in the earth. Our emotions can show the joy of God, the grievance of the Spirit, the urgency of the hour. The emotions can express the anger of the Lord or the peace He extends to the troubled mind.

EMOTIONAL SOURCES

When we break it down, our emotions can come from two sources: the unregenerated man or the born-again, Spirit-filled man. Our emotions are an outburst from one of the two.

When emotions come from the unregenerated part of man, they are carnal. They oppose the Word of God. They want to be in control. Because the world does not understand Spirit-led living, they operate entirely by their emotions and intellect. According to the world, it is fine to do whatever feels good. If someone wakes up one morning and does not feel a positive emotion for his mate, he leave her. If having an illicit relationship feels good, he does it. If he doesn't feel like showing up for work, he doesn't go. His life is in constant confusion because his emotions are always going up and down.

The emotions also fluctuate up and down in the believer. The only difference is the spirit man has the final say in the matter, not the emotions. As believers, if our emotions rule us, we cannot stay in communion with God. A *prayer is not answered on the basis of emotion.* Prayers receive answers when we speak from the unction of our spirit man, according to the Word.

> **If our emotions rule us, we cannot stay in communion with God.**

Our emotional realm wants to rule our lives whether we are born again or not. When we have a personal relationship with Jesus Christ, He becomes the rudder of our souls. When He guides us, our emotions must line up with the Word. They are not allowed to trick us in things contrary to Scripture. This is where the enemy attacks us as believers.

EMOTIONAL ATTACKS

If we have not yet learned that our emotions are sub-servient to our spirits, we are open territory for the attacks of the enemy. When the enemy cannot gain entrance into our wills, he will head for our emotions. If he can get our emotions to follow him, the attack will cause our wills to weaken.

A sure sign of an emotional attack is in the area of self-pity. When we have been hurt or wounded, the emotions pull to the forefront. During an attack, we first react by withdrawing under fire for protection. When we withdraw, the harness falls off our emotions, allowing them to rule us. When self-pity becomes the basis from which we view everything, the enemy is wreaking havoc on us. When self-pity rules us, our view becomes warped. We feel that everyone opposes us and no one likes us. We begin to feel that everyone else is wrong and we are right.

Self-pity moves over into arrogance, which is an area of pride. Arrogance is the soulish way of protection. Many who have been hurt wear arrogance as a covering to hide their wounds. When we wear that false cloak, we cut off the blessings of God into our lives. We cannot hear His voice when He prompts us to move for Him. Even if we hear Him, we cannot break out of the sheath of arrogance to be obedient.

When anger dominates your life, every action you put forth will produce strife.

The use of self-pity and arrogance is only one way the enemy rules in our emotions. Remember, he plans to ruin our destiny in the earth. *If he can render us immobile through our emotions, then our spirits cannot follow God effectively.*

Another area through which the enemy attacks our emotions is anger. If we have been hurt by another and refuse to obey the Word of God, then anger can rule us.

When anger dominates your life, every action you put forth will produce strife. Revenge becomes your utmost desire. Anger causes your emotions to revert to an adverse stage. Instead of living in the righteousness, joy, and peace of your spirit, emotional anger produces a wilderness. It causes you to feel isolated and alone. Just as in the natural wilderness, you move to hurt whatever crosses your path because you are afraid; so it is in this emotional realm. You only rejoice if those who hurt you suffer hurt themselves. Anger will eat away at you like a cancer. It's never satisfied.

Anger operates in bitterness, and if we continue to let the enemy rule our emotions in this area, we will never fulfill the plan of God in the earth. When we allow the enemy to successfully gain ground in our emotions, we act as a carnal man. The Bible says a carnal man acts as if he has never known God or His ways. (See Romans 1:18–32.)

Our emotions are not equipped to see into the realm of the spirit. The eyes of faith are gone when emotion leads us. We are only moved by what we see in the natural. If we are only motivated by what we see in the natural, the devil will make sure we see and hear a lot.

Emotions will cause us to look for negative support. Gossip and slander surface, and we find ourselves in total confusion. We no longer trust anyone and would rather live our lives alone. That is how the enemy keeps his hold in the emotional realm. His whole plan is to keep your will from wanting the things of God.

EMOTIONAL FREEDOM

How can we break out of an emotional attack? By forcing our emotions to be silent and trust the Word of God no matter what happens around us.

As we have previously discussed, the book of Psalms provides a great disciplinary book for the soul. Amidst trouble and calamity, David forced his emotions to be subjected to the

Word of God. He continuously said phrases like, *"Oh Lord, open thou my lips; and my mouth shall show forth thy praise"* (Psalm 51:15); *"Make me to hear joy and gladness"* (verse 8); *"I trust in the mercy of God for ever and ever"* (Psalm 52:8); *"I will hear what God the LORD will speak: for he will speak peace to his people"* (Psalm 85:8); and *"Why art thou cast down, O my soul? and why art thou disquieted within me? hope thou in God: for I shall yet praise him, for the help of his countenance"* (Psalm 42:5).

Once I understood the spiritual implication of the attack against me and the purpose of it, the book of Psalms became an outlet for me. The words David spoke came alive as never before. I spoke some of these same words to God for my very life, just as David did.

Notice that, in every Scripture I just gave, David was taking control of his emotions. It didn't matter who was wrong or right in the circumstance he was dealing with. What mattered was how David *himself* would deal with it. The trouble outside of him was bad enough; he couldn't afford to cave in with it. David had enough wisdom to know the trouble would pass. He could take his experience and live in bitterness or move on into wisdom and strength. We can see from his life that he chose the latter.

The situation you may face today is much the same. We all face emotional attacks. The point is to understand the purpose and goal of the enemy. Once you understand according to the plan of God for your life, you are in position to make your emotions line up to the Word of God. You can easily open anywhere in Psalms and read the correct response to a vexing attack. As you read these psalms, begin to express them with your own cry to God. Before long, your emotions will silence themselves and your spirit will take supremacy.

When that happens, what you see will no longer move you. If your emotions try to tempt you, line them up with your spirit man. The enemy will have no doorway to your emotions if you seal them with the Word of God.

CHAPTER

7

SEVEN

THE INTELLECT
UNDER ATTACK

The human brain is extraordinary. No scientist or medical doctor is able to explain how a small mass of tissue can retain and understand knowledge. Human intelligence is unexplainable to science because God created it to function in His image.

Human intelligence, in the wrong vein, can be an enemy to the works of God. Although intelligence is a wonderful thing and should be sought, the world has made intelligence into its god and used it as the sole means of survival.

To the world, intelligence places humankind in class categories. It does not see all men as equal. If someone doesn't think the way our class does, then they are called uncivilized or barbarian. According to God, the very opposite is true. *God sees men according to the heart, not the intellect.*

God placed intelligence inside of us to help us understand the workings of God and to cause prosperity to abound in the earth. Mixed with the Spirit of God, intelligence accomplishes great feats. No matter what culture we are in, if we prosper in

226

that environment, intelligence has served us. For example, I doubt a city businessman could survive in the wilderness for very long. Yet the people who live in the wild, outside of an office building, would be labeled incompetent. The world has widely misused its definition of intelligence.

GODLY INTELLIGENCE

To the believer, intelligence works with our spirits to cause understanding. God desires to reveal Himself to us and have us know His ways. In the book of Isaiah, we read,

> *Come now, and let us reason together, saith the* LORD: *though your sins be as scarlet, they shall be as white as snow; though they be red like crimson, they shall be as wool.* (Isaiah 1:18)

God delights in our using intelligence to understand His ways. The Hebrew interpretation for the word *reason* also means to "decide, convict."[1] Our intelligence has a part to play in conviction and submission to God. The Bible says only a fool would say, *"There is no God"* (Psalm 14:1).

God desires to reveal Himself to us and have us know His ways.

It is the will of God for a believer to turn his intelligence into godly wisdom. Proverbs 19:8 says, *"He that getteth wisdom loveth his own soul."*

Intelligence will turn into godly wisdom if we mature our souls according to the Word. Proverbs also says that the Lord *"layeth up sound wisdom for the righteous"* (2:7) and *"happy is the man that findeth wisdom"* (3:13).

---

[1] James Strong, *The Exhaustive Concordance of the Bible* (Nashville: Abingdon, 1890) "Hebrew and Chaldee Dictionary," p. 49, #H3198.

The Bible says that the earth was formed by wisdom, and that wisdom's price is far beyond rubies or gold. Godly intelligence produces peace and security. It is a safeguard from destruction and poverty.

NATURAL INTELLIGENCE

Natural intelligence resists God because it wants to rule in His place. Natural intelligence thinks it is wiser than God and chooses to set up rules and regulations to prove it.

The theory of evolution came from an intelligent mind. It reasoned our existence far beyond the limits of the available information and came up with its own source for humanity. Natural intelligence has figured everything out. It worships logic to the point of disregard for anything supernatural. Miracles do not exist to the natural intellect. By relying solely on the natural intellect, one cannot see the purposes of God. The Gospels aren't logical; they are spiritual. Intelligence must remain submitted to the reality of God if it is to be of true and honest use.

> **The Gospels aren't logical; they are spiritual.**

On the other hand, many have set up religious rules and regulations for multitudes to follow. They reason that you cannot serve God unless you do such and such on such and such a day. In the Bible, the Pharisees and Sadducees were good examples of intelligent men who reduced their service to God down to works alone. They gave no worship and service from the heart. If an act contradicted tradition, it upset their intelligence and they rejected it.

Although natural intelligence has accomplished tremendous feats, it cannot be the only source from which we draw knowledge or truth. Our spirit man is to be the prime function of our being. God intends our intelligence to follow the leading of our spirit. The two combined will produce accuracy in every feat we attempt. It is in the area of this relationship between spirit and intellect that the enemy begins his attack on human intelligence.

ATTACK ON INTELLIGENCE

Remember, the enemy's goal is to dethrone God from His rightful position in your life. He will trick you and deceive you in any way he can to accomplish his goal. How can you tell when your intelligence is being attacked?

First and foremost, logic overrides the inward witness. Then your faith and belief in God begin to fade. Sadly, most cults of the world started because of a leader who was attacked in his mind and didn't recognize it.

You may be going on your way, living your life as usual, but the thoughts come: *God isn't real. There is no such thing as healing, deliverance, etc.* If you listen to them, you'll begin to intellectualize everything you see. The enemy sets you up in thinking you are being superior and objective, but really you are playing the fool. Before long, you feel cold and dead inside. You don't want to pray and you objectively criticize the Word of God piece by piece. You certainly will not tolerate the preaching of the gospel. You find yourself with an opposing statement for each sentence you hear from the pulpit.

If you don't fight this attack, you will begin to look at the local church as a bunch of weak, dependent, low-life people who need a crutch in life. If you've gotten to this stage, you'll find the only things that motivate you are success-oriented exhortations that stimulate your intelligence.

COMMON SENSE

Another area of attack is in our common sense. If the devil cannot get you to question and act upon the existence of God, he'll try to get you to quit using common sense.

I heard a preacher say once, "Why is it when some people get born again, they seem to throw out their common sense?" God expects you to use common sense mixed with the promises of His Word.

For example, there are those who confess healing Scriptures all day, but then they go outside in subzero weather without a coat. They don't take care of their bodies and diet. Then they expect the blessings of God in the areas of healing.

> **God expects you to use common sense along with the promises of His Word.**

Then there are those who constantly speak prosperity on themselves but never look for a job. Yes, it is true that God provides for the sparrow; but even she leaves the nest to get the worm!

There are also those who have families and assume each member knows how much they are loved, simply because they are "provided for." But these people never take the time to express their love and care to others. As a result, that family never knows they are truly loved. Their children turn to other things for acceptance.

Do not be deceived in the area of common sense. Do not take important details for granted. Do not look at the Word of God as a "cure-all" when you have not done your part as well. The principles of God are not magic. Instead, they are principles of faith, and faith requires some action on your part.

Godly faith, mixed with inspired action, will overcome any obstacle in your path.

HOW TO RECOVER

If you are under this attack and have believed it, the first step in recovery is *repentance.* Ask the Spirit of God to make Himself real to you and show you His works. Many have told me that, almost instantly, the Lord has quickened their memory of His works and set them free.

Ask Him then to soften your hardened heart and to give you new eyes and new ears to see and hear His Word. Force yourself to be at every meeting of your church. It doesn't matter if you want to go or not—*be there.* God will see your faith in action, and it will count as righteousness to Him. One day you will walk into the meeting and the Spirit of God will melt your heart. He will restore and solidify His ways in you, and you'll leave a new person. Remember that your heart was not hardened overnight. You cultivated the attack against you for quite a while to be in such a condition. Give the Spirit of God a chance to work with you.

> **Ask God to soften your heart and give you new ears to hear His Word.**

Begin to be involved in your church's outreaches. You don't have to go with the evangelism team right away; work as a door greeter or book table worker. Force yourself to be friendly and reach out to the people of God. Purpose to be vulnerable to the message from the pulpit. Ask God to show you how it applies to your life. He will not fail you or leave you hanging. Begin to tithe again and support the work of God. God will prosper you and show you the work of His hand.

You must command the spirit of unbelief to leave you in Jesus' name and have no hold on you. You must take spiritual authority over the harassing, tormenting spirits sent to vex your thoughts. God is real; and it is far better to go to heaven serving Him than to die believing He is only a crutch.

Begin to fellowship with those who are strong in the Lord. Those who walk in godly strength will not condemn your temporary weakness. They will exhort you and live a victorious life in front of you. They will sharpen you as you gain strength and will be a balance for you. Pray for godly friends such as that. The Bible says in Psalm 119:63, *"I am a companion of all them that fear thee, and of them that keep thy precepts."*

Surround yourself with those who fear the Lord, for that is true wisdom and intelligence. Seek after godly intelligence. The Bible says in Psalm 111:10, *"The fear of the LORD is the beginning of wisdom: a good understanding have all they that do his commandments."*

You do not have to lose your destiny with God. You do not have to fall subject to the enemy through pride and a hardened heart. Recognize his attack against you and stand your ground. If Jesus tarries His coming, the generations following you will gain from your strength and determination. You are valuable to God and His plan.

CHAPTER
8
EIGHT

THE IMAGINATION
UNDER ATTACK

The human imagination is a part of the soul, yet vastly different from the other parts. We have the ability to imagine beyond our intelligence. For example, we can imagine something and still not intelligently put it together. We might envision a goal or a dream and still not have the intelligence of knowing how to get there.

To me, the imagination is a very spiritual part of the soul. It is one of our most valuable assets. I love a person who has imagined a dream and has put it into action. Our imagination has the creative ability to do anything for God and can build creations that humanity has not yet seen.

When we do not understand how the principle of imagination must be united with action, we will dream our life away. Faith is not fantasy. Idle imaginations alone cannot produce anything, physically or spiritually.

When I was a young boy, I was aware of the call of God on my life. I would read my Bible, pray, then shut myself in my room. I had a huge map of the world on the wall. I would

233

stand in front of it and preach to it. I would point with my finger to different places and say, "I'm coming to you!" That was my godly imagination, envisioning the plan of God for my life. *I didn't stop there though.* That map of the world isn't just paper hanging on my wall; it is now the ground of nations I have visited.

Imagination without well-timed action is fruitless. It is heartbreaking to hear the godly imagination of a person then watch them sit and do nothing toward it. Ten years later, the person may come to you with the same vision, maybe greater, yet he still works at the corner store.

When combined with well-timed action, imagination is a powerful force.

Imagination is a powerful force. When combined with action, in God's timing, imagination changes nations, cities, churches, and communities. It originates in your thought life. Imagination is very important to God. If you can see something in your imagination, it is within your reach. In Genesis 11:6, the Word says,

> And the LORD said, Behold, the people is one, and they have all one language; and this they begin to do: and now nothing will be restrained from them, which they have imagined to do.

Although this passage arose from a negative vein, the principle here is the same. Because the people were of one heart, they could do whatever they imagined! Their imagination had no limits for them. From this Scripture we can see that our abilities have nothing to do with our intelligence. Our ability stems from our imagination and our willingness to see its work accomplished in the earth.

As a matter of fact, intelligence can hinder imagination. Imagination works for those who dare enough to believe it and who will stop at nothing to see it work. Imagination comes from a desire in your heart. This is why your imagination will reveal the hidden secrets of your heart.

IMAGINATION OF DAVID

Although imagination is a force, it cannot produce by itself. It cannot come about by speaking something into existence. Imagination comes about by action. Let me give you a biblical example.

In the book of 1 Samuel, we read the story of David and Goliath. David used the principle of imagination in his slaying of Goliath. When he went out to face the giant, he had envisioned in his head what would happen. Goliath attempted to intimidate him, but David's vision overpowered the giant's words:

And the Philistine said to David, Come to me, and I will give thy flesh unto the fowls of the air, and to the beasts of the field. Then said David to the Philistine, Thou comest to me with a sword, and with a spear, and with a shield: but I come to thee in the name of the LORD of hosts, the God of the armies of Israel, whom thou hast defied. This day will the LORD deliver thee into mine hand; and I will smite thee, and take thine head from thee; and I will give the carcases of the host of the Philistines this day unto the fowls of the air, and to the wild beasts of the earth; that all the earth may know that there is a God in Israel. And all this assembly shall know that the LORD saveth not with sword and spear: for the battle is the Lord's, and he will give you into our hands. (1 Samuel 17:44–47)

David imagined it, put it into action, and it happened just that way.

GODLY IMAGINATION

What constitutes the working of a godly imagination? Reality or unreality. We have the ability to imagine in either vein.

When a heart is submitted to the plan of God, all its imaginations are overflow from the Spirit of God. The plan it envisions furthers the kingdom of God and turns the hearts of humankind toward heaven. *There is no self-exaltation in godly imagination.* True imagination inspired by the Spirit of God is almost humbling. Once we've seen it, we understand it is a reality that we can never attain without the strength of God.

> **True imagination inspired by the Spirit of God is humbling.**

THE ATTACK OF UNREALITY

The enemy works in our imagination by getting us to exalt ourselves. These imaginations are envisioned in the same way, but find themselves in unreality. If we are not wise to their source, we can follow them and wake up in shambles.

In Genesis 3, Satan used the principle of imagination on Eve. He showed her the fruit and caused her to imagine its taste and texture. He knew the fruit was forbidden to her. The unreality set in when she was told in verses 4 and 5,

Ye shall not surely die: For God doth know that in the day ye eat thereof, then your eyes shall be opened, and ye shall be as gods, knowing good and evil.

She imagined that eating the fruit would make her equal with God. She envisioned it and took her husband with her. They ate it and were cursed. They fell into the trap of the enemy through their imagination.

That is what Paul told us:

Casting down imaginations, and every high thing that exalteth itself against the knowledge of God, and bringing into captivity every thought to the obedience of Christ.

(2 Corinthians 10:5)

Imaginations that exalt themselves over the Word of God are not from heaven. Sometimes we are deceived into thinking that any feat accomplished comes from God. That is not true. The end results and the lasting effects show what spirit it comes from. The believer may have had good intentions but remained ignorant that the enemy was attacking all along the way.

If the enemy cannot get us to imagine selfish dreams, then he will try to turn those for God into self-exalting imaginations. You must guard against those attacks and seek to bring God glory in everything you do. How can we be deceived into self-exalting imaginations?

There are several ways. One comes from pride. Another, from undisciplined flesh. Still another, from past hurts and wounds.

But a point I want to bring out is in the area of fantasy. The world offers a variety of creative fantasies. In this troubled generation, multitudes are searching for a way to escape the pressure. As a result, we have movies filled with fantasy. We have amusement parks and novels laced with fantasy. But the Bible warns us concerning the excess of fantasy and fables. If we feed them continuously into our minds and hearts, then our imagination will reflect them.

The Word says,

And they shall turn away their ears from the truth, and shall be turned unto fables. (2 Timothy 4:4)

For we have not followed cunningly devised fables, when we made known unto you the power and coming of our Lord Jesus Christ, but were eyewitnesses of his majesty.
(2 Peter 1:16)

Neither give heed to fables and endless genealogies, which minister questions, rather than godly edifying which is in faith: so do. (1 Timothy 1:4)

> **Faith is not fantasy. It is a force that always produces.**

An unhealthy exposure to fables, or fantasy, can cause us to lose our purpose. If we have been hurt, wounded, or attacked, the enemy will tempt us to indulge in fantasy as a way of escape. Before long, our godly imaginations will be tainted by unreality.

Notice that the Word does not say that having fun is wrong. We can have fun, but we must also deal with reality. Instead the Word says that "turning away from the truth" toward fantasy, following fantasy, or giving heed to fantasy is dangerous. It opens the door for the enemy to confuse you. The mind is impressionable. Those who are hurting must be careful not to hang on to fantasy and embrace it as a way of life. Fantasy causes us to exalt ourselves, and we will lose our accuracy in the things of God. Remember, faith is not fantasy. Faith is a substance and a force that always produces.

Fantasy also causes your imagination to become passive. If your imagination is passive and empty, something will surely come to fill it. If the whispers of the enemy fill our minds, we will end up following them. Passivity of mind and imagination creates an area of danger for the believer.

If you overindulge in fantasy, you will become mentally depressed. People who live in a fantasy world do not face the real issues of life. One day they wake up and find their life has gone nowhere. They are so grieved and mentally depressed from it that some commit suicide. These same people may have everything going for them. The problem was that they allowed their imagination to be manipulated by the devil through fantasy

HOW TO RECOVER

Protect the imagination that God has given you. Be aware of the schemes of the enemy. Keep your heart humble before the Lord. Guide your imaginations into their proper channels by the Word of God. You are unlimited in what you can accomplish for the kingdom of heaven. God wants you to have a creative imagination. Do not let it go in the wrong direction. Line every imagination against the Word of God and ask yourself, *Is God exalted or I alone?*

If every believer would operate in the godly imagination offered to him, we would literally change the entire world for God.

CHAPTER

9

NINE

THE MEMORY
UNDER ATTACK

The human soul is a great entity. Every part of it expresses the character and personality of God. We have discussed the human will, the emotions, the intellect, the imagination. Although each area could have an entire book written on it alone, we have discussed the key concepts enough for you to find stability in these areas.

The last area of the soul is extremely important as well. The memory serves as our point of reference in every thought we have. Every scene we visually see, every thought we have, every word spoken to us, everything we read, everything we eat—anything that crosses our path—is automatically stored in our memory. The human memory is fascinating! It is so valuable that when people lose it through injury or disease, they no longer know who they are. They can no longer recognize once familiar sights. Although they still have a will, an intellect, an imagination, and emotions, they have lost their identity as a person.

Memory has the power to conduct our way of life. For this very reason, *your memory also must be ruled by your spirit or you cannot successfully fulfill the plan of God.*

DAVID'S POWER OF MEMORY

Let's go again to 1 Samuel 17. The life of David can show us the power of using our memories to fulfill God's plan. We have already discussed how he used his imagination to slay Goliath. Now let's look at how he used his memory to bring him courage.

And Saul said to David, Thou art not able to go against this Philistine to fight with him: for thou art but a youth, and he a man of war from his youth. And David said unto Saul, Thy servant kept his father's sheep, and there came a lion, and a bear, and took a lamb out of the flock: and I went out after him, and smote him, and delivered it out of his mouth: and when he arose against me, I caught him by his beard, and smote him, and slew him. Thy servant slew both the lion and the bear: and this uncircumcised Philistine shall be as one of them, seeing he hath defied the armies of the living God. David said moreover, The LORD that delivered me out of the paw of the lion, and out of the paw of the bear, he will deliver me out of the hand of this Philistine. And Saul said unto David, Go, and the LORD be with thee.

(1 Samuel 17:33–37)

David relied on the power of his memory to give him the courage to believe God. He remembered how God had been with him in past trouble. Because of that great victory, he knew God would be with him in this feat as well. His memory ignited his faith, and he conquered the giant without fear. That is the way God created memory. He designed it to bring

241

into remembrance the good things in life and the Word of the Lord, to cause us to remember the faithfulness of God. Our memories can bring an unflinching trust in the plan of God.

PAUL'S POWER OF MEMORY

Paul said many similar things in the New Testament. One in particular is found in his second letter to Timothy:

Notwithstanding the Lord stood with me, and strengthened me; that by me the preaching might be fully known, and that all the Gentiles might hear: and I was delivered out of the mouth of the lion. And the Lord shall deliver me from every evil work, and will preserve me unto his heavenly kingdom: to whom be glory for ever and ever. Amen.

(2 Timothy 4:17–18)

Paul also relied on the power of his memory to give him courage to fulfill his mission on the earth. He remembered that if God delivered him from evil before, He would do it again.

He also admonished Timothy to remember the prophecies that were spoken to him:

This charge I commit unto thee, son Timothy, according to the prophecies which went before on thee, that thou by them mightest war a good warfare; holding faith, and a good conscience; which some having put away concerning faith have made shipwreck. (1 Timothy 1:18–19)

In 2 Timothy we can read another exhortation to our memory:

Wherefore I put thee in remembrance that thou stir up the gift of God, which is in thee by the putting on of my hands.

For God hath not given us the spirit of fear; but of power, and of love, and of a sound mind.   (2 Timothy 1:6-7)

From these verses we can see that, if we stir up our memory for God, we will move in faith rather than fear. We will operate in power and godly love. Our godly memories cause us to retain a sound mind. All through the Word of God, we are exhorted to remember

Godly memory causes us to retain a sound mind.

the stability from which we came and to live by it. If we can understand the positive attributes of a memory submitted to the Word of God, then we will see how the enemy attacks us.

ATTACK ON THE MEMORY

If the enemy can harass and torment your memory, he will paralyze you. It is that simple. I have seen men and women fall because of bad memories. When we have been seriously hurt from an enemy attack, it stays in our memory. If we do not deal with these memories and effectively recover from them, we will make life decisions based upon them. They will cripple our personalities.

That is a terrible way to live. If we think about it, why should we base our lives on the hurts and wounds of the past? We must remember this important statement: *The future is not based on the hurts of the past.* Everyone has been hurt and wounded at one time or another. *We cannot base the outcome of our futures on past disappointments or past victories.* If we don't break free from that "claw," the enemy will direct our steps.

The devil uses our memories as an art gallery. He will cause similar painful circumstances to surround us, then say, "Remember how that hurt you? Let me walk you through the gallery of your hurts. See that? Remember this?" If we listen to it, we will succumb to fear.

Fear causes withdrawal and paranoia. If the enemy has good access to our memories, everyone we meet will be sized up according to our hurts. We will fear to trust anyone. How can we walk in unity if we remain "an island to ourselves"? How can we thrust out into the confidence of God if we mistrust all those called to help us? We cannot hide behind fear for very long. It is like a fire that burns inside of us, destroying the influence of God.

Fear produces death, disease, and torment. Faith produces life, health, and peace.

Fear is the force Satan operates through, just as faith is the power that moves heaven into the earth. Fear robs us of the faith of God. If faith produces life, health, and peace, then fear produces death, disease, and torment.

Fear robs you of a good conscience. Maybe you did something wrong. Maybe you gave in to carnal sin. Even though you have repented and even though, according to 1 John 1:9, you were absolutely forgiven, the enemy will attempt to rob you through your memory. When you go to pray for the sick, he will remind you of a sin, as though it was not forgiven. If you put that memory before the Word of the Lord, you will feel unworthy to be used by God. As a result, the sick will not receive the benefit of your prayer.

If you sinned against another person, a natural reconciliation is necessary also. Many times, that alone will shut the mouth of the enemy. But if you have done everything you know to do and harassment still persists, then begin to condemn what is condemning you. Reverse its effect and verbally condemn the torment with your mouth in Jesus' name! If you allow the mental abuse to continue, your conscience will be marred. When a memory robs your good conscience, you lose effectiveness. You have a sense of unworthiness and inferiority. You feel insecure in everything you do, and it will show. That, my friend, is a memory under attack.

Paul said a godly memory produces love. The opposite is true when the memory is under attack. A tormented mind produces hate and hardness. It operates in impulsiveness, trying to escape the torment of a bad memory. A tormented memory suspects evil in every person. It covers itself in a false pride. Because it operates from fear instead of faith, it has lost hope and cannot help others in trouble. If we nourish and feed the flesh when our memory is under attack, we will seek our own exaltation rather than wait for the righteousness of God. A memory under attack, distorted by fleshly self-exaltation, has lost confidence and trust in God.

If we operate in this category for very long, we will lose the soundness of our mind. Mental wards are filled with hopeless victims, put there from unforgotten hurts and wounds. When soundness of mind goes, many complications set in. Medical science attempts to administer peace to the patients, but in many, the sole cause was a hurt left unresolved. Medication will not heal the hurt; it can only paralyze a memory.

We must fight for the power of our memory by the Word of God. *If God tells us repeatedly to remember His Word, then the plan of the enemy will cause you to forget it.*

HOW TO RECOVER

Command the tormenting spirits to leave your memory. Purpose to forgive again those who have hurt you. Begin to look past the hurt into the faithfulness of God. He wants to work on your behalf. If hurts have not entered in and sinful memories are harassing you, then find Scripture to fight back. For example, in the Old Testament, Job fought an attack by this: *"I made a covenant with mine eyes; why then should I think upon a maid?"* (Job 31:1).

Job chose to covenant with his eyes, the mirror of his memory, that he would monitor what he looked upon. Purpose in your heart to do the same.

Do not allow the devil to rob your destiny through fear. Fight back!

Maybe you have been paralyzed by fearful stories and events. Perhaps the enemy has reminded you that the same outcome will be in your life if you follow God. Fight back! Do not allow the devil to rob your destiny through fear. When David was afraid of his future due to stories of the past, he said,

> *Deliver me, O LORD, from mine enemies: I flee unto thee to hide me. Teach me to do thy will; for thou art my God: thy spirit is good; lead me into the land of uprightness.*
>
> (Psalm 143:9–10)

Whatever situation you face, the Word of God provides a sound cure for it. We must realize that the future is what I call "virgin territory." No man has yet walked into it. The future is bright and does not have to be tainted by what we have already lived through. Isaiah 43:18–19 speaks specifically of your future: *"Remember ye not the former things, neither consider the things of old. Behold, I will do a new thing."*

The apostle Paul said in Philippians 3:13–14,

But this one thing I do, forgetting those things which are behind, and reaching forth unto those things which are before, I press toward the mark for the prize of the high calling of God in Christ Jesus.

Paul recognized the power of his memory, good and bad. He made a statement in those verses *that spoke loudly to his soul.* He emphasized that, no matter what else he accomplished, his first priority was to forget the things that lay behind him and press on into the future.

As leaders and believers, we must set our faces like flint and refuse to subject ourselves to the past. All of heaven will work with us in our endeavor. Attitudes such as that attract the power of God. It draws strength and power into us. It produces invincible faith and will move mountains.

You have the authority of your memory. You will choose the thoughts you meditate on. You were sent to the earth for a purpose. Do not lose it from a careless memory. *Gird up the loins of your mind, and conquer the ground placed before you!*

CHAPTER

TEN

THE HUMAN BODY UNDER ATTACK

Though the enemy can attack the soulish parts of a human being, that is not the end of his battleground. The human body is also a prime target, and it can be as greatly hindered as the soul of man.

The human body is our natural flesh, tissues, blood, membranes, organs, and nervous system. God gave the human body, His handiwork, for us to live in and to carry the gospel into the nations. When we see acquaintances on the street, we recognize them by their human forms, or when we hear their names, we visualize their human forms in our minds. Each human body was created as an individual. Although some are identical twins, no one is created exactly alike.

Carnal people idolize the human body. They do not look past the flesh and understand who the real person is. I have traveled all over the world, and there are statues in every major city, idolizing a male or female physique. In the natural, people often base their selection of a mate on physique. If people give in to their carnal instincts, the human body has the power to turn them into fools.

Even though we recognize another person by their outward appearance, their body is not the real person. It is merely their shell. The real person is the spirit man. The spirit man is eternal and lives forever. The body that so many idolize will die. Our bodies house our spirit man. The human body keeps the spirit man on the earth to fulfill the will of God. If your body dies, the spirit leaves. It cannot stay.

YOUR BODY AS A VESSEL

Your human body is the vessel by which the Spirit speaks and moves. Your body is the vessel by which the gospel is carried into the nations. Many times, God chooses to heal the afflictions of another *through* your human hands. He chooses to speak His revelations *through* your mouth. He desires to express His presence *through* your bodily presence in a room.

The human vessel has always been important in the plan of God. In the book of Acts, Stephen understood this principle. He yielded his body to the Spirit of the Lord and allowed his voice to be used to convict those around him. The religious leaders of the day had resisted the influence of the Holy Spirit up to that point. But the Word states in Acts 6:10, they could not resist the Holy Spirit's influence when He spoke through a human vessel, Stephen.

Jesus wants to live through our human bodies. He wants to come out and show His strength and compassion to the world. He desires for the Scriptures to come alive through our mortal flesh. He took the time while on earth not only to show us the power in overcoming the soul but also to pay for the afflictions of our bodies. Not only did He take the sins of the world with Him to the cross, He also took the diseases and sicknesses of the body. He shed His blood, paid for them, and pronounced healing for all who would believe Him.

God desires the Scriptures to come alive through our flesh.

If we do not take care of our physical bodies, our time on the earth can be cut short. Many great ministers of the past died early because they neglected their physical bodies. *Our bodies were not created only for our pleasure, but also for the service of the Lord.* In spite of all the medical terminology for the functions of the human body, if we can understand this one principle, then we can know the reasons for spiritual attacks against it.

ATTACK ON THE HUMAN BODY

The enemy attacks the human body in two ways: by sense and by sickness. The human body houses five different senses: *sight, smell, sound, touch,* and *taste.* If these senses aren't modified, the devil will use them to tempt us into extremes. The attack against our senses comes in the form of temptation. If we live a loose lifestyle and something looks tempting, smells nice, or feels good, then we can fall into sin. If we are unguarded, the sound of something can stimulate the human body to sin.

Television, billboards, magazines, and other materials stimulate the body's senses. *If the enemy cannot attack you successfully in your soul, he will aim for your senses.* We must be careful what we gaze upon and what we listen to. When the flesh yields to these distractions, it cannot please God. Guard your senses, as they are the entrance to your body.

The human body is a seeker of its own pleasures. It knows no limits. It will go after anything, and it doesn't know when to stop on its own. Every craving the body has must be controlled.

The second way the enemy attacks the body comes through sickness and disease. The devil wants to hinder our labor for the Lord and even destroy our flesh to get us off the planet. He does not want the power of God revealed through our bodies. If he cannot destroy our souls, he will attempt to devastate our flesh.

Guard your senses, as they are the entrance to your body.

Jesus hates sickness and disease because it destroys our bodies. He is not intimidated by it, nor does it influence His power. He hates it because it hurts humanity. Part of the Great Commission in preaching the gospel is to heal the sick and all manner of disease. Jesus spent a large portion of His earthly ministry healing the sick. He heals because of His love and compassion toward us. He does not want the human body to suffer.

When someone has been under attack mentally for a period of time, it may begin to spread in his human body. Sometimes the enemy will use symptoms that seem real but cannot be medically explained. This is nothing but an attack on the physical body.

HOW TO RECOVER

Do not give in to the manifestations of these attacks! Stand against them, and call them for what they are. Be led by the Spirit: Do something contrary to these symptoms. Call upon the resurrection strength of the Lord to come into you. Command pain to go, and refuse to let it enter. Many times fear is the spirit that keeps these symptoms working in you. I have talked with many people plagued by migraine headaches. One in particular said that each time one came, he checked himself to see if he feared something. When the area was discovered, he rebuked the fear, and the pain left immediately.

Don't let the devil torment your time of rest and sleep. Calm your thoughts and speak peace to them.

Quote the Word of God:

I will both lay me down in peace, and sleep: for thou, LORD, only makest me dwell in safety. (Psalm 4:8)

If the enemy can rob your rest, he will gain entrance into your soul. Many people have fallen into sin due to lack of rest. You must take care of the physical man through good eating habits, exercise, and rest. You cannot work all the time and keep your mind buzzing when you should be sleeping. If you are physically tired, it is hard to gain spiritual strength. In the book of Daniel, part of the job of the enemy is to *"wear out the saints"* (Daniel 7:25). *It is the will of God that you rest, sleep, and renew yourself.*

> **God heals because of His love and compassion toward us.**

If you need a physical healing from actual disease in your body, then keep believing the Word of God. (See Isaiah 53:5.) Listen to anointed preaching of the Word that professes and believes in the healing power of God. Read testimonies of healings. Build up your faith to receive God's best. (See Psalm 1:1–3 and Romans 10:17.)

God desires that we give our bodies to Him as a living sacrifice. (See Romans 12:1.) This isn't a dead, lifeless sacrifice, but a living, healthy one. He desires the willful control of our bodies and our senses. He wants to live through them and show the world His love and power. In Philippians 1:20, Paul had this to say:

According to my earnest expectation and my hope, that in nothing I shall be ashamed, but that with all boldness, as always, so now also Christ shall be magnified in my body, whether it be by life, or by death.

Becoming dead to your flesh does not mean that life will cease to be exciting. Allowing Christ to live through your human body is the most thrilling experience on earth. Do not allow the enemy to cheat you from knowing Christ's life through you.

CHAPTER
ELEVEN

THE HUMAN SPIRIT UNDER ATTACK

The spirit man is the direct channel between God and ourselves. We receive instruction, direction, and purpose from our spirit man. We follow the unction of the Holy Spirit in our spirits and direct the rest of our lives from the warnings we sense from it.

The spirit man is the primary seat of our entire being. We were created spirit first, then body and soul. Although your spirit man follows the same commandments that every other believer follows, it is still an individual. Each spirit man has a different call and a different function to make the body of Christ complete. Your spirit man will express itself to the degree you submit to God. Your spirit man is unlimited in potential and purpose. It feeds and nurtures itself from the Word of God.

Proverbs 20:27 says, *"The spirit of man is the candle of the* LORD.*"*

Our spirit man is the light of God to the world. For this reason, the spirit must affect your soul and your body. The

Bible did not say your emotions or your flesh was the light of the world. The Bible says Jesus, from your spirit man, is the Light to the world. Your soul and body only reflect the light of your spirit and express it.

Although being filled with Jesus helps us become the candle to the world, it is still our choice whether or not to let it shine. The Bible clearly states that *"if we live in the Spirit,"* we must also learn to *"walk in the Spirit"* (Galatians 5:25).

As believers, once we are born again, we must learn the operations of our spirits according to the Word of God. We must learn the character of God Himself and the movements of our spirits toward Him. We must learn how to abide by the spirit and how not to quench its actions. We must learn to base our decisions upon the unction within us and follow them. As we discipline ourselves to the workings of our spirits, we will become strong in spirit and will be useful to the purpose of God.

We must learn God's character in order to become strong and useful.

The enemy attempts his attack in this area.

ATTACK ON THE SPIRIT MAN

As we have already discussed, the enemy tries first for the soul and body of man. His purpose is to shut off the outlet we have of expressing Jesus to the world.

But when a man is spiritual, and the body and soul are totally subject to his spirit, then the attack will hit the spirit man immediately. If the man is ignorant of the devices of the enemy, he will succumb to his tactics. Is it possible for a man to have his body and soul subjected to the Word of God and still be ignorant of the attack on his spirit? Yes!

Even while disciplining your flesh and soul, if you have lost your joy, your liberty of expression, and your spiritual perceptions, then your spirit is under attack. Some of the most sincere believers, adamantly trying to renew their minds in the area of body and soul, have lost their sense of righteousness. They have feelings of total unworthiness and base the discipline of their bodies and souls on that feeling. What was once an exciting spiritual frontier, has now become a "box." They have lost their vision.

You must understand that the main function of the spirit man is revelation. The spirit man is the highest creative power inside of you. Revelation should abound in every form of your walk with God. Revelation should come to you in every area: from the lost on the street corner, to the depths of the Word.

LOSS OF ACCURACY

In true guidance from the Spirit of God, your human spirit and renewed, mature mind work together. Your spirit gets the plan and unction, and your mind agrees with the Word of God in the situation. The guidance is not impulsive, and your intelligence is not in constant rebellion to it.

> **In guidance from the Spirit, your spirit and renewed mind work together.**

We must be careful when we think our minds will be in constant disagreement with the Holy Spirit. When we think this way, our common sense leaves us. It is true that the law of God is spiritual, but that is the reason we are constantly *renewing* our minds to His Word. When we receive instruction from the Holy Spirit, if our minds have been renewed in the Word, then our minds will *submit* to the Word and the plan. Even if the mind does not understand, if it has been renewed, it will agree in *faith* with the plan before it.

There will be certain situations that call for a quick and seemingly impulsive response or action. These situations usually mean life or death, and the mind doesn't have the time to think. We move in these situations from the prompting of the Holy Spirit through us. But in the long-range plan of God, the renewed mind must be in a faith agreement with the Holy Spirit. When we shut our minds off, we open ourselves to a driving spirit.

When a person is driven, he is out of cooperation with God. A driven person is trapped in a never-ending cycle. Being in his presence is exhausting. Even his words weary you. He begins to look old and tired far ahead of his years. (The quickening Spirit of the Lord causes youthfulness to come and brings life to your flesh.)

Being spiritually driven is extremely dangerous. If someone is driven, he is under attack. If he is under attack, portions of his life will not add up according to the Word of God. Dangerous deception enters in right here. Just because he had success in one area, he expects others to assume *every area* of his life is also led by God. When a person is driven, he is exceptionally hardened to human needs and desires. As a result, he becomes a taskmaster and insinuates that everyone is to follow that direction or they are not following God. This attack of the enemy is not only centered to destroy the driven vessel but countless others as well.

SPIRITUAL WISDOM

We need to understand that since we are spiritual, we are open to the entire spiritual realms—good and evil. Just because something comes to us spiritually, that does not mean it is from God. We must line up every thought and unction according to the character and Word of God. If we think every thought and unction comes from the Spirit of God, then we are setting ourselves up to be infallible and are sure to be misled.

How can we know if our spirit man is under attack? *If the plan or purpose we feel pulls us out from a deeper fellowship with God, it is from the enemy.* It doesn't matter how good it seems. It doesn't matter how much it promises or how much potential is there for a great work. If our fellowship with God decreases because of it, it is not from Him. To fulfill a true unction from God, we must rely on a constant relationship with Him to complete it.

Since we are spiritual, we are open to good and evil in the spiritual realm.

If your spirit is depressed and has lost joy, peace, creativity, and liberty, it is under attack. When you feel an overwhelming unction to act emotional and frenzied, your spirit is under attack. When you are driven beyond normal means, and your fellowship with God is sidetracked by a "spiritual" desire, you are under attack.

If you are in this area of attack, then get back to basics. *Refuse* to be driven. *Refuse* to let your fellowship with God be sidetracked. *Refuse* to let impulsive desires take action. Learn to season yourself with the Word under the authority of good leadership.

The greatest need in the church is to know and understand the laws of the Spirit. Fully maturing your spirit man produces accuracy in your cooperation with God. The loss of spiritual accuracy has hurt every move of God in the earth.

When you get caught up in the movings of God and refuse to take time to mature your spirit man, revival will be short lived. Strong and stable accuracy must come forth.

Take time to invest in your spirit man. Not only will it cause you to fulfill your life destiny, but the end results will inspire maturity in everyone you meet.

CHAPTER

TWELVE

THE RECOVERY ZONE

The purpose of this book is to alert us to the different areas of attack. In the past, we have been too vague in the area of spiritual battles. Most believers know they are under attack, but they cannot describe it. It is important that we learn to discern accurately where we are being attacked and why. If we can understand the area, we will know how to effectively recover.

In conclusion, there are just a few points I want to leave with you.

After we've stood and won a spiritual war, *we still need time to recover.* Know that. Sometimes we say, "Hallelujah! It's over!" and think we can run the race at the same pace as before. We think everything is over and we can go right on as before. *Many who have successfully won during the attack fall backward during recovery.*

Why? They don't understand that *it takes time* to build strength again. Or they think because they aren't quite as sharp as before, they are still in a war. They fight something that isn't there. Finally, they're worn out and discouraged. They just give up.

Just as your body needs to recover from a physical illness, it must also recover from a spiritual attack. Think for a minute. After the initial sickness is gone from you, and you feel better, you can't run a marathon yet! The sickness is gone, the battle is over, but your body needs time to regain strength. The same is true in the spiritual realm. Don't rush yourself. Let God have time to work for you. Give yourself room to grow and mature in the things you have been through.

Remember not to overestimate or underestimate the war you have gone through. It is commendable that you made it; give God the credit and use the wisdom it has produced in you. God likes to encourage you, so let Him. Encouragement aids in your recovery and healing. Allow yourself to be the son or daughter of God, and let Him be a Father to you. It's good to hear Him talk to you and point out what the two of you did together. Let Him do it and rejoice with Him.

> **Just as your body needs to recover from illness, it must recover from spiritual attack.**

Remember these other basic points of recovery:

1. Pray in tongues.

The *Amplified* version of Jude 20 says it best:

But you, beloved, build yourselves up [founded] on your most holy faith [make progress, rise like an edifice higher and higher], praying in the Holy Spirit.

I like that translation because it paints a picture of what faith mixed with praying in tongues can accomplish. An *"edifice"* is a structure. *Merriam-Webster's 11th Collegiate Dictionary* defines it as "a large or massive structure." *Your faith, kindled by the Word and by praying in tongues, causes you to rise and solidify yourself into a mighty, towering force.* (See 1 Corinthians 14:4.) No wind of doctrine or controversy can shake you when the two are combined within you. When you build yourself up by prayer and the Word, your house will stand when trouble comes. Your fervent prayer avails much. (See James 5:16.)

2. Sit under a good anointing. Feed on the Word—the Bread of Life.

When you are recovering, the Word of God delivered under a good anointing is like cool streams of water to you. Understanding and revelation come when the preaching is clear and sharp. You'll hear God in new dimensions when you sit yourself under a leader who hears from heaven. Read and devour the Word of God. It will strengthen and feed you, making you strong and unconquerable.

3. Worship God in the privacy of your devotion time.

This is not the time to be silent. Lift your hands, open your mouth, and praise the Lord! Dance before Him (see Psalm 150:4), and receive the joy of His strength into your being. When you worship in spirit and truth, it enables you to walk above circumstances and controversy. Then join yourself with the congregation of the saints, and pierce the heavenlies with strength and praise.

4. Confess the Word.

Find the Scriptures that speak directly to your heart in this time of your life. These Scriptures mean life for you. Speak them out of your heart and allow them to transform your thinking and circumstance. The Word of God was designed to fight and take pressure from you. It promises to complete the mission

God sent it to do. It will never return void or incomplete, and it will prosper in the areas it speaks to. (See Isaiah 55:11.)

5. **Have someone pray for you. Your friend's prayers can add to your recovery.**

Your most trusted spiritual friend knows how to pray for you. The Bible says that one can put a thousand to flight, two can put ten thousand away. (See Deuteronomy 32:30.) Why do alone what two together can accomplish?

6. **Listen to good gospel music and read good gospel books.**

You don't always have the time to sit, read, and pray. Thank God for CD players! Put in a good gospel CD and allow it to minister to you as you go about your daily work. Instead of reading the newspaper or a popular magazine, read the story of a great man or woman of God. Read about their trials and temptations and how they overcame them to complete the plan of God. Read books on faith, healing, or deliverance. Allow good gospel books to supplement the Word of God in your life and add to your understanding and application.

7. **Fellowship with good Christian people.**

This subject is so deep, I could write another book on it alone! Find the people who uplift and encourage you. Surround yourself with those who know how to laugh and bring godly joy into your life. Fellowship with those who have the same morals, the same fervency for God, and the same purpose. Friends who fear the Lord bring a good balance into your life. Through the right associations and connections, your life can be enhanced and sharpened like iron. (See Proverbs 27:17.) If you don't have any godly friends, ask God to bring them into your life. He will never fail you.

ABOUT THE AUTHOR

Roberts Liardon, author, public speaker, spiritual leader, church historian, and humanitarian was born in Tulsa, Oklahoma, on February 14, 1966, the first male child born at Oral Roberts University. For this distinction he was named in honor of the university's founder. Thus, from the start of his life, Roberts was destined to be one of the most well-known Christian authors and orators of the twentieth century. To date he has sold over six milliion books worldwide in over fifty languages and is internationally renowned.

An author of over forty Christian and self-help books, Roberts' career in ministry began when he gave his first public address at the age of thirteen. At seventeen he published his first book, *I Saw Heaven*, which catapulted him into the public eye. By the time he was eighteen years old, he was one of the leading public speakers in the world. Later he would write and produce a book and video series entitled *God's Generals*, which became a best-selling Christian series and established Roberts as one of the leading Protestant church historians.

Roberts' eminence increased outside Christendom as well. Twice he was voted Outstanding Young Man in America, and his career has taken him to over one hundred nations. He has been hosted by presidents, kings, leading political and religious leaders, as well as other world dignitaries. He has had the pleasure of meeting the likes of Billy Graham, former President Ronald Regan, and former Prime Minister Margaret Thatcher, and he received a letter from President George W. Bush honoring him for his commitment and contribution to improving the quality of life in his community.

In 1990, at the age of twenty-five, Roberts Liardon moved to Southern California to establish his worldwide headquarters in Orange County. There he founded Embassy Christian Center, which would become a base for his humanitarian work, including assistance to the poor and needy in Southern California and throughout the world. As part of his ministry, he also built one of the largest Christian churches and Bible colleges in Orange County. He has established, financed, and sent over 250 men and women to various nations on the globe. These humanitarian missionary teams, which take with them food, clothing, medical supplies, and spiritual teaching, provide expertise and assistance to those in need.

Overall, Roberts Liardon has paid the price for his accomplishments in prayer to God and service to mankind. He has dedicated his entire life to putting his finances to work for the kingdom of God and welfare of his fellow men, keeping a watchful eye on those less fortunate and doing all he can to ease their pain and help their dreams come to pass.

ROBERTS LIARDON MINISTRIES

CONTACT INFORMATION

United States
Roberts Liardon Ministries
PO Box 30710
Laguna Hills, California 92654-0710
E-mail: info@robertsliardon.org

Indonesia
Impact Indonesia
PO Box 1731/JKs 12017
Jakarta Selatan-Indonesia
E-mail: rlmindonesia@yahoo.com

Mongolia
Operation Mongolia
PO Box 985
Central Post Office-13
Ulaanbaatar, Mongolia
E-mail: operationmongolia@yahoo.com

Philippines
RLM Philippines
PO Box 80131
Bankgkal Davao City
8000 Philippines
E-mail: slbcasia@dctech.com.ph

South Africa
Roberts Liardon Ministries
PO Box 3155
Kimberley 8300, South Africa
E-mail: crc@crc-kimberley.org.za

Sharpen Your Discernment
Roberts Liardon

We all know people whom we would call wise, prudent, or discerning. What sets these individuals apart is their ability to walk in the guidance of God. Do you feel like you receive direction from God? You can! Author Roberts Liardon sets you on the path to pursuing a life marked by wisdom. With the knowledge and insight found in this book, you can find out how to be led by the Spirit of God, develop a plan of action for successful decision-making, defeat the spiritual forces of evil in your life, and discover the immense power in daily prayer and Bible-reading. *Sharpen Your Discernment* and you will become more than a conqueror!

ISBN: 0-88368-988-X • Trade • 176 pages

W
WHITAKER
HOUSE

proclaiming the power of the Gospel through the written word
visit our website at www.whitakerhouse.com

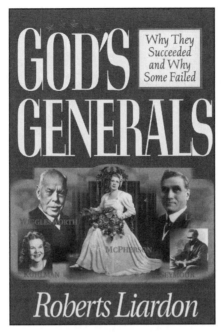

God's Generals:
Why They Succeeded and Why Some Failed
Roberts Liardon

Some of the most powerful ministers ever to ignite the fires of revival did so by dynamically demonstrating the Holy Spirit's power. In these fascinating pages, Roberts Liardon faithfully chronicles the lives and spiritual journeys of twelve of *God's Generals,* including William Seymour, the son of ex-slaves, who turned a tiny horse stable into an internationally famous revival center; Aimee Semple McPherson, the glamorous and flamboyant founder of the Foursquare Church and the nation's first Christian radio station; and Smith Wigglesworth, the plumber who read no book but the Bible—and raised the dead!

ISBN: 0-88368-944-8 • Hardcover • 416 pages

WHITAKER
HOUSE

proclaiming the power of the Gospel through the written word
visit our website at www.whitakerhouse.com

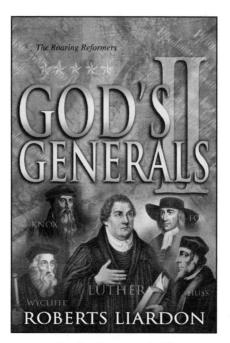

God's Generals II:
The Roaring Reformers
Roberts Liardon

The basic truths of the Protestant faith—the things you believe
and base your life on—were not always accepted and readily taught.
Here are six of *God's Generals* who fought to reestablish the core
beliefs and principles of the early church in an atmosphere
of oppression, ignorance, and corruption that pervaded the
medieval church. As you read about these *Roaring Reformers*,
men who sacrificed everything in their fight for God, you
will appreciate the freedom you have to worship and find
encouragement for your spiritual battles.

ISBN: 0-88368-945-6 • Hardcover • 416 pages

UI
WHITAKER
HOUSE

proclaiming the power of the Gospel through the written word
visit our website at www.whitakerhouse.com